WISCONSIN COUNTRY COOKBOOK
AND JOURNAL

By Edward Harris Heth

Illustrated by Arlene Renken

Tamarack Press
P.O. Box 5650
Madison, Wisconsin

To the friends
who have helped me collect these recipes

First published by Simon and Schuster, Inc., as *The Wonderful World of Cooking*. Reprinted by Tamarack Press by permission of the Estate of Edward Harris Heth and Larry Sternig Literary Agency.

Printed in the United States of America by George Banta Company, Inc.

Library of Congress Cataloging in Publication Data

Heth, Edward Harris.
    Wisconsin country cookbook and journal.

    First published in 1956 under title: The wonderful world of cooking.
    Includes index.
    1. Cookery, American—Wisconsin. I.   Title.
TX715.H5735 1978   641.5'9775   78-21695

ISBN 0-915024-20-9

CONTENTS

Contents

Contents

Rare Beef with Sauce—Leftover Beef or Steak Croquettes—Spaetzle—Silesian Liver Dumplings—Cottage Cheese Dumplings

—Dill Pickle Soup—Lopscush—Chicken and Onion
Soup—Black Bean Soup—Lentil Soup with Prunes—
Corn Chowder—Beer Soup—Chicken Liver Dumplings
—Veal or Chicken Forcemeat Balls—Beef Dumplings

INTRODUCTION

by
Euell Gibbons

Here is a book that titillates the appetite and captures the soul. For *The Country Kitchen Cook Book* is far more than a cookbook. It is a manual on living the good life. And a very versatile manual it is, adaptable to many times, places and circumstances. You needn't live in a country house on a hill to share Edward Harris Heth's joy in the changing seasons and his perfect understanding of the context of a meal as well as its content. His feeling of harmony with the countryside is a quality of the book that I, as a countryman, find particularly attractive. But wherever you live, you can relish the delicious food he serves forth—perfect meals for the first warm days of spring, or a lazy summer's day, or a cool autumn evening, or a snowbound feast.

The author is a modest man and doesn't demand that you slavishly follow his directions, but encourages you to flout his recipes or adapt them to your needs and opportunities. Part way through the book I had to stop reading and head for the kitchen. Hours later, stuffed with Ham Horns, Onion Pie, and Mushroom Salad, I was eager to return to Mr. Heth and his company of characters— the odd and amusing and wise and colorful neighbors he serves up with his glorious food. Best of all, he serves up himself. A good writer naturally and unavoidably puts himself into his work, and Mr. Heth, all unconsciously, reveals his great heart opening up in a wonderful way to the world about him, the people he meets, and to you and me, his readers.

The author has a refreshing attitude toward cooking and food. I am an incurable devourer of cookbooks, and in the flood of such books pouring from the presses today one encounters many odd attitudes toward eating. Some are diet books that consider food a danger and a menace, an enemy that can't quite be conquered, but which must be confined, emasculated and ruled with an iron hand. Such food doesn't have character; it has calories, and meals made of it are little more than so many carefully counted digits. Closely related to the dieters are some of the health-food enthusiasts who seem not to eat food at all, but to ingest nutrition, carefully compounded of exact quantities of vitamins, minerals, carbohydrates, proteins and fats. At the other extreme are some of the modern gourmets who think of food chiefly as a status symbol, a means of impressing others with their esoteric knowledge and sophisticated tastes. And, even in this affluent age, we still have the economizers, those who want us to feed our families on chicken backs and turnip soup and save up to a dollar a week on the food bill. Very popular right now is another kind of economizer—the "instant"cook whose sole aim seems to be to save work and time in the preparation of food.

To Edward Harris Heth good food and drink—yes, and their painstaking preparation—are among the amenities of the good life. He doesn't save time, he spends it joyfully and recklessly, and he feels he receives full return for each moment spent at this creative art.

Some of his recipes, such as Morel Bisque, Partridge in Vine Leaves, and Broiled Squab with Oyster and Fruit Stuffing, are authentically gourmet. But this is not just a cookbook for well-to-do epicures. By using produce from his own garden, and by the clever utilization of those free gifts of nature such as fish, game, wild fruits and wild vegetables, Mr. Heth eats in glorious fashion for less than most of us spend for the mundane fare we choke down. Most modern, work-saving cooks buy altogether too many fancy packages of prepared and half-prepared foods, and this is an expensive way to feed a family. Mr. Heth buys his groceries in an unprepared state, not to save money (although it does that, too), but because he wants all the preparation to be under the direction of his own keen mind, loving heart and skillful hands. It would easily be possible to spend twice as much for food and still not eat half so well as did the family and guests in the House on the Hill.

How healthful is such rich fare? What could be more nutritious than tender vegetables snatched from one's own garden at the very moment they reach perfection, or tangy dandelion greens and wild asparagus plucked from God's own organic garden? Mr. Heth's food is prepared with love and shared and eaten with joy, and I believe that those intangible nutritional elements, love and joy, are more essential to health than all the vitamins and minerals in the book. But won't such fine food tempt us to overeat and gain unwanted pounds? There are two ways to lose weight. One is by eating less and the other is by exercising more. Catch your own fish, dig and hoe in your garden, find and gather your own wild fruits and vegetables, then spend hours of joyful time and pleasurable work in bringing the dishes you create from these precious ingredients to perfection, and you will expend enough energy to burn up all those extra calories.

When Mr. Heth writes on wild food he is getting into a territory with which I am very familiar, and I like his approach. Writing on wild food is enjoying a boom, but far too many of these modern primitives seem to think of wild food as an economy for the poverty-stricken or as emergency survival fare for the lost hunter or downed airplane pilot. Such writing maligns some of the finest food in the world, relegating my beloved uncultivated food plants to the role of second-choice substitutes for supermarket items and implying that one would eat wild food only as an alternative to starvation. By contrast, Mr. Heth considers these wild delicacies ornaments to his cuisine, adding taste thrills that can't be purchased at any price. Such writing restores to wild food the reputation and prestige to which its fine flavors and innate goodness entitle it.

Edward Harris Heth's point of view is that of a nature lover, not a nature tourist or a sentimental sightseer who admires nature from a safe distance. Living in easy intimacy with his garden, the fields, woods, lakes and streams of southern Wisconsin, he begins his creative encounters with nature before the last snow is completely melted, when he and Matt Barker tap the maple trees on the hill for the essential ingredient in Maple Dumplings. They continue through Dandelion Salad, Cream of Wild Asparagus Soup, Mulberry Pie, Wild Blackberry Roll, Spiced Wild Gooseberries, Wild Blueberry Pickle, and Veal with Wild Plums to Hickory Nut Torte and Pickled Butternuts. All the recipes in this book, wild or tame, are arrayed in chronological order as the seasons roll by, and especially in the area of wild foods this arrangement proves sheer genius. To be absolutely perfect each dish must be eaten in its proper season.

Of course the book doesn't make maximum use of the wild food possibilities of southern Wisconsin, but I don't demand that others be as enthusiastic about *my* hobby as I am. While reading these rhapsodies on the delectable morsels that nature offers in that section of the country there were times when I felt like shouting a few bits of glad news. He sings the praises of Sorrel Soup even while bemoaning the fact that French sorrel is seldom planted in home gardens and is almost impossible to find in the markets. He considers this soup so outstanding that he includes two Sorrel Soup recipes even though he thinks that most of his readers will be unable to obtain the most essential ingredient. Right here I can be a bringer of good tidings. Wild sheep sorrel, *Rumex acetosella*, which grows literally everywhere in this country, is a close relative of the cultivated kind, identical in flavor and just as good in every way. Anyone who will take the trouble to learn to recognize this exceedingly common wild plant can usually find all the sorrel he can use. Even the slightly larger French sorrel, which Mr. Heth praises so highly, has gone wild in this country and has become thoroughly naturalized along the Canadian-U.S. border. I have picked this tame-sorrel-gone-wild from New Brunswick to Minnesota.

However, the common wild sheep sorrel is just as good as the cultivated kind, if not actually better, and it is far more available. I once picked a handful of this sorrel from the flower boxes in Rockefeller Center, where it was growing as a weed. It can be found in parks, back yards, in waste places, on vacant lots and along many waysides. Unlike many wild vegetables, sheep sorrel has a long season, being usable and delicious from mid-spring until after autumn frosts. I have used wild sorrel in both Mr. Heth's Sorrel Soups and they were superb. I did make a slight change in his Hot Sorrel Soup the second time I prepared it. I banished the turnip for trying to steal the show. Its flavor dominated entirely too much for my taste, and I thought the soup better without it.

Another place where my desire to interfere becomes overpowering is when Mr. Heth has an inner debate about which dish he will prepare to celebrate the arrival of spring, considering, among others, Dandelion Salad and Wild Asparagus Soup. These two wonderful wild foods can never compete for my attention for chronological reasons. I go on a dandelion orgy during the very first warm days of spring, almost as soon as the ground thaws enough for my knife to reach down into it and slice off the crown of the dandelion root, an essential part of this magnificent vegetable. At this time dandelion greens are crisp, sweet and entirely satisfying, but the buds on the perennial roots of the wild asparagus have scarcely started to swell. I consider the dandelion season over when their yellow flowers begin to appear, and this happens before the first wild asparagus shoot peeps above the ground. True, dandelion greens are still wholesome and edible during wild asparagus season, but they are altogether too bitter for most tastes at that time. Incidentally, dandelion dishes can also be used to celebrate the arrival of Indian summer, for these delectable wild plants again become sweet and palatable after experiencing a few freezes and some frosty nights in the autumn.

I hope that I am not giving the impression that one must be a wild food enthusiast to enjoy this book. The sheer joy of life leaps from these pages, whatever the subject, as when Mr. Heth writes of his dinnerless dinner parties where the hearty hors d'oeuvres consist of one savory culinary creation succeeding another until dinner becomes redundant. There is smile-provoking whimsy when the guests discuss menus they would like to serve to People You Can't Stand with a main dish of Weiners Stuffed with Peanut Butter in Lime Gelatin. Never has the term "belly-laugh" been more appropriate. There is even macabre humor here, when Aunt Dell refuses to cook the customary baked ham for a funeral feast, because the dead man had hated pigs—so she cooked roast loin of pork instead, and her roast pork was such a treat that not one of the neighbors pointed out her inconsistency.

I found nostalgia here, for my mother also knew the secrets of the dill crock, and some of the most pleasant memories of my childhood are of fishing in that fragrant brine for dilled green beans, cauliflower florets, tiny pickled onions, tangy dilled green tomatoes, and, when I felt especially adventurous, taking a clove of the garlic that had been put in to season the other things, or even nibbling on a flower of the pickled dill itself. There is no reason why the composing and ripening of the perfect dill crock should become a lost art. Do I have plans for that ten-gallon crock that has been sitting empty in my cellar? Yes, and for that little two-gallon one also, for some dilled vegetables can only achieve perfection in company with others while some need solitude to ripen properly.

In only one area do I find this book a failure. It simply won't do as bedtime reading. I tried it several times and each time, after an hour or so spent in Edward Harris Heth's country kitchen, reading and salivating, I would get up and head for my own country kitchen where I would spend more hours preparing and consuming some of his more toothsome concoctions, to the great detriment of both my rest and my waistline.

PART ONE

THE GREEN SPRING

CHAPTER ONE

SPRING COMES QUICKLY

DOROTHY WORDSWORTH WROTE to Coleridge that spring came slowly up her way (it was the middle of the month of May), but here among the Welsh Hills of southern Wisconsin spring blows in overnight. For months the hardwood trees have been standing in their long shadows. But for the last few weeks there has been a lightening of the hills, an intimation of something about to lift. Unawares, you walk with an easier tread when you step outside. The willows are yellow tossing stalks, and the native dogwood, or osier, is a bright tangle of red twigs. While you still fear another snowfall, a few rains come instead to cleanse and soften the earth, a few winds blow away the fumes of winter. Another day dawns that you think will be just another day (the sky brightens earlier than you expected, too) and a hot sun comes striding over the meadow and there is spring.

It is all insistence to leap from the earth, unfold, nourish you. The dock and milkweed shoots are up along the fence-rows for Aunt Dell to collect for her salads. The radishes and peas, sown impatiently last fall, sprout in wavering rows—at least mine always waver—before the vegetable garden has

3

been properly spaded. It is planting time. The soil begs for seeds. A wise gardener and cook, whether he has an acre or the smallest city plot, will choose his seeds carefully: carrots that grow slim and tall, not the tub-sized giants, though catalogues recommend them. Midget corn. Bibb and Boston lettuces, by all means, and the packets of solid-headed iceberg thrown away, with its size and texture of bowling balls. Brussels sprouts and tomatoes and green and yellow beans chosen from the catalogues for their promise of succulence rather than for productivity and hugeness.

Even the smallest garden can support one hill of zucchini, which is all an average family will need. A sunny corner, even a window box, will hold a plant apiece of the important herbs, sweet basil, thyme, sage, rosemary, chives, tarragon. A row of parsley—or better still, chervil, though it is more difficult to grow—can trimly encircle a pansy bed. No country garden should be (yet most in the North are) without an ample supply of greens for steaming or for use in spring and summer salads—mustard, kohlrabi, spinach, Swiss chard and beets. The beetroots themselves I'd happily see stay underground all their lives and after, unless a few small ones are dug to cook along with the beet greens. And no garden, country or city, should be without at least one plant of the neglected, perennial and marvelous French sorrel. It is an endless pleasure in hot or cold soups, stews and salads.

Planting done, you'd think a man could lie back for a few weeks and wait for the garden to produce its bushel basketfuls of green and red and yellow wonders. But I am always tormented by trying to decide *what* I will eat first, from garden or field or woods or neighbor's poultry yard, to make me know that spring has officially arrived. A potful of Spring Soup with its flecks of shredded greens floating among the cream and lemon slice? A chicken slaughtered and broiled almost before it is able to walk? Or slim, sharp, white radishes, chilled, sliced lengthwise thinly and salted to make them sweat, which are wonderful with Martinis drunk on the terrace in an early May dusk while it's still really too chilly to be sitting there? Or dandelion greens, gathered from the meadow, tossed in a salad with crumbles of bacon as my grandmother used to make it?

Each year I think it is the dandelion salad that will win. Spring makes me remember my grandparents, who lived near here, and childhood visits to their farm. I can inhale again the odd scent of soapy dishwater tossed from a gray enamel dishpan over gray stones under a blooming apple tree in my grandmother's yard. Just as vividly I can smell again the violets and trailing arbutus that crammed homemade paper May baskets, hung on a neighboring girl's front doorknob while the shy donor raced frantically away to hide. And each spring my nostrils prickle again at the lovely sharpness of lemon and vinegar, plus a little bacon fat, being trickled over the young dandelion greens. Perhaps these remembered fragrances helped to draw me away from New York City after a long stay there, back to my native state, to build a house and slowly settle, as though for a lifetime, among these low, shadowy hills.

But each year before I have got around to gathering the pale-green-and-white dandelion leaves, on a bright mid-May morning an ancient limousine rolls up the hill to the house. And I know the case of the dandelion salad has been lost. It is Aunt Dell, my neighbor from the village, who is approaching, and at sight of her I know it is neither chicken nor radish nor salad that will announce spring to me. The herald will be Aunt Dell's Cream of Wild Asparagus Soup.

"Get yourself a hat on and a basket, mister," Aunt Dell says, grinning hugely as she descends from her high, second-hand limousine. "Time we hunt us up some wild asparagus, ainna?"

In spring neighbors emerge like animals burrowing out of winter torpor. They will come from surrounding farms or the village. Some, like myself, are former city dwellers who have built new homes or remodeled old ones to live year round in the country. Before long there will be the summer crowd too, though now their sprawling homes around the many lakes nearby are still shuttered and locked. It is a comfortable, interwoven neighborhood, and as we begin to see each other more often and easily after a sleepy winter, a busyness awakens over the countryside, not unlike nature's own busyness in fields and woods. No neighbor is so busy, or welcome, as Aunt Dell. She is a product of sun and spring and ripening summer. She actually grows huger and happier each year as the corn grows fatter.

Her real name is Adelaide Dell and she is not really anyone's aunt ("except," as she says with a cheerful jab of her thick thumb, "to some of my own relations, see?") but everyone calls her Aunt Dell. She is a tall and joyous woman with a passion for hugeness in everything surrounding her—her house, her garden, her secondhand limousines, and in her own family. You are never sure how many children there are since, besides her own eight or nine or ten, her house and table are always crowded with the neighbors' children plus, if she can manage it, the neighbors themselves as well as any passers-by on her shady street.

Her table stretches vast and white, crammed with two or three roasts and a dozen relishes and vegetables for an ordinary supper—and yet Aunt Dell moaning that she had nothing in the house. But she is a natural cook. And on a warm, blowy spring day she will arrive to lead me through the wooded hills, breathless from trying to keep pace with her as her ample body swings first here, then there, gathering leaves and shoots and fiddleheads that I had not even known existed before. She can spy the tender, prodding shoot of a wild asparagus from a distance of fifty feet. Her basket laden, we return to the kitchen—water rushes from faucets, pots and kettles clang, spoons rap and tap; and soup, springtime, and a neighbor like Aunt Dell become highly valued blessings.

CREAM OF WILD ASPARAGUS SOUP

This recipe might serve four, or Aunt Dell and me. With the soup there will be the crusty rolls she has brought along, sometimes with cold ham sandwiched in them, and fresh berries for dessert.

Cut 2″ tips from 1 lb. asparagus, using those from your own garden or vegetable store if the wild ones are not available. Steam the tips in as little water as possible until they are tender, about 7 or 8 minutes. To 1 qt. of chicken or veal stock, or 4 cups of water and 4 chicken bouillon cubes, add a few leaves of spinach, a few fresh tarragon or ¼ t of the dried, a stalk of parsley and a pinch of coriander, and the asparagus stems. Simmer half an hour. Add salt and freshly ground pepper. Slice 4 scallions thinly, including the green tops, and fry until golden (no longer) in 2 T butter. Sprinkle with 1 T flour, stir well, add the boiled asparagus stems and cook 5 minutes more. Mix all this with the boiling stock and cook 10 minutes—it should reduce slightly. Rub through

a sieve or food mill. Add 1 cup good cream in which an egg
yolk or two has been stirred, and lastly the asparagus tips.
Heat but do not boil and sprinkle lightly with powdered
mace, which contributes an elusive, springlike flavor.

After the first shower during a warm May night Aunt
Dell also appears to wander along the edge of the woodland
or through hills not too densely overgrown to search for
morels. These honeycombed, pyramidal, beige mushrooms
appear by magic overnight, coaxed by warmth and rain and, I
suspect, by incantations from Aunt Dell, for I have never
been able to find them on my own. They are as vagrant and
stealthy as gypsies when I search for them, but she will travel
the same paths I have traveled and come home with a basketful. But she is, luckily for me, incapable of not sharing her
richest treasures ("and they don't keep good anyway, see?"
she says, grinning, as though her busy presence and clatter
around my stove needed apology); for lunch on those days
she will fry the sliced morels in butter with a bit of fresh or
dried sweet basil, with much brisk shaking of the frying pan
and then a final squeeze of lemon; or interweave them gently
between the folds of an omelet, all in a delicate blanket of
cream sauce made with country cream so full-bodied and
golden that little flour is needed to thicken it. After lunch on
one such morel-gathering day she leaned back comfortably in
her chair, folded her stout, bare arms, sighed hugely and
spoke my own thoughts: "Beats all, ainna?"

It was the day she had prepared a morel bisque. Of necessity I must substitute what she calls store-bought-and-boxed
mushrooms when I want to prepare it, but it remains one of
the best soups I've eaten.

₰ MOREL (OR MUSHROOM) BISQUE

Chop ½ lb. fresh, cleaned mushrooms, caps and stems, into fine bits. Fry 3 or 4 minutes in 3 T butter. Add 1 shallot, thinly sliced, or 2 chopped green onions, along with a handful of greens—spinach, sorrel, young dandelions, any one or in combination, including a bit of parsley—all of which must be shredded as fine as new blades of grass. Simmer 5 minutes longer. Sprinkle with ½ t celery seeds, salt and pepper, ¼ t caraway and add ¼ cup dry white wine. Simmer another minute, then combine with 1 qt. boiling chicken stock, and be sure to scrape every last morsel out of the frying pan. Cook 15 minutes more, not too gently, and thicken with 1 cup cream mixed with 2 egg yolks. Heat only, and serve with a slice of shaved lemon and dash of paprika in each bowl, and a dish of very small fried croutons.

There are soups for winter and soups for spring. All fresh, light, cream soups, their flavors as gentle as the breeze brushing against the iris, seem particularly right for lazy lunching outdoors under the arbor where the white grape is unfurling its sweet, spicy bloom. You smell the grape bloom, sip the equally fragrant soup, glance toward the rock garden where the grape hyacinth is blossoming deep blue against the pink phlox, sip again the velvety soup. A lifetime could pass this way. Since I have been living in the country, an easy-to-prepare soup called Spring Soup has evolved by trial and error.

₰ SPRING SOUP

This is a soup of great variety and one that calls for the experiment and invention that all good cooks enjoy. The base, however, is always the same. Slice 2 large potatoes, an onion, a carrot, and a turnip, and fry only until golden in a generous amount of butter. Combine the vegetables with 1 qt. rich chicken stock or bouillon and boil until the vegetables are tender enough to pass through a sieve or food mill.

Now search the garden for its freshest, most tender greens. Bibb or Boston lettuces, endive, watercress, young Swiss chard, spinach, tiny flags of beet greens—any of them may be used. You will need about 2 cups, cut up into thinnest ribbons. Add this to the stock and sieved vegetables and simmer for 10 minutes, along with 1 t finely chopped fresh herbs such as chervil, basil or rosemary (if only the dried are available, add them when first cooking the broth). Add a little cream if you like. You should have a very smooth soup, with floating strands of varicolored greens which, by the way, present an eating hazard since they will dribble down your chin. Don't salt the broth too highly or you will lose the subtle flavor of the greens and herbs; grind fresh pepper over the soup when it is taken from the fire. Either add 2 or 3 cooked fresh shrimps to each bowl or top with 1 t sour cream sprinkled with a few drops of lemon juice or grated lemon rind and chopped chives.

Iced cucumber sticks are good with this, or ham or mushroom horns. I was taught to make these by a Russian neighbor who calls them *piroshki*. At least he was pretending to be out of Chekhov at the time.

ࣸ HAM OR MUSHROOM HORNS

The above-mentioned neighbor, Alfred Lunt, says you need not be an expert at pie dough to prepare these, because the crust must be rolled so paper-thin that you cannot tell whether it is tough or not. Cut the rolled pie dough into 4″ squares; on each, place 1 large t of the following mixture:

Grind up some boiled ham or leftover baked ham or use the deviled canned ham, and season to taste with wet mustard. Or for the ham substitute mushrooms and mince them after frying 3 minutes in butter. Moisten either the ham or mushrooms with soft butter or cream or leftover gravy, if the latter is not too heavy in flavor. Add some chopped fresh dill if it is ripe, otherwise a small amount of finely chopped dill pickle. Salt and pepper gently. Spread on the squares of crust, roll up like a jelly roll, starting from a corner, shape into horns, brush with egg yolk, and bake in a moderate oven until the crust is done.

There were other neighbors besides Aunt Dell to become acquainted with and grow fond of, after moving out here, and two of these from the village were Matt and Rosalie Barker. There was a long autumn and winter of exchanging shy nods and furtive, brusque hellos at the village grocery store or when we met at the corner filling station, before I was invited to their neat yellow house for dinner one spring evening. It was, in fact, to be a party—an unhappy one for Matt, I think, though we have since become fast friends. The party would celebrate the birthday of one of the village teachers, Miss Schneider, who bakes the famous Schoolteacher Pie. A few other neighbors had been asked, Aunt Dell had brought Rosalie with her one day to pick asparagus along my road, and in a burst of the friendliness that springtime generates in the country, I was invited too.

Since it was to be a party we were to eat in the cheerful, wainscoted dining room. This was no unusual occurrence but what was unusual—and to Matt heretical—was that for the first time in his thirty married years he found Rosalie's plate at the head of the table, while his own was far away at the foot. Matt is six foot three, a bald-headed man, gentle for his size. He stands firmly and, if necessary, belligerently on his own feet. But this unexpected distance between Rosalie and himself appalled him.

In the country, even for company or holiday dinners, a man's rightful place at table is beside his wife, for her to watch that he is properly fed. For thirty years this is precisely where Matt had eaten every meal, with Rosalie protectively at his elbow. But this evening (out of deference to a guest who had just moved into the community from New York, Rosalie told me later when we had become easy friends) she and Miss Schneider had put their heads together and agreed that it would be pleasant to seat guests in a more sophisticated fashion. Rosalie at the head. Matt at the foot. Miss Schneider on his right. I on Rosalie's. Cheerful, talkative neighbors in between, all husbands separated from their wives.

Rosalie has a firm set to her lips when she has reached decisions, a lovely flush, and a warm twinkle in her eye. Grayhaired, wearing a pretty flowered dress, she seated herself calmly at the head of the table. At the same time Matt began reaching for the chair toward which she had motioned me.

"No, Matt, you go down there," Rosalie said softly. "You sit at the foot, across from me."

Matt paled. He was stunned. "Way down there?"

"Yes, Matt."

"But, dammit, Rosalie, what'll I *do* so far away?"

"Now, now," Rosalie soothed, but all of us could see the sudden, grateful tears in her eyes, "you just take your place like I tell you. I'll just look down at you every once in a while, and there's nothing that's going to happen to you."

"*You'd* never know, twenty feet off," Matt grumbled, but dutifully, and miserably, took his proper place.

It was halfway during dinner that he upset the gravy boat. Matt leaped angrily to his feet to face Rosalie. "You see!" he roared. "What'd you expect? Me here—and you way off there!"

At that springtime party I first tasted a sugared leg of young lamb, of which Rosalie is justly proud, with its excellent gravy and heightened flavor. A good cook knows instinctively what foods complement each other: with the lamb there was garden spinach, lightly bathed in sour cream (and tasting so fresh and green it seemed to have left the earth only a moment before it appeared on the spotless table) and also golden, crisp, roasted new potatoes—two vegetables that are also delicious with very rare leg of lamb, as another friend prepares it.

৽ SUGARED LEG OF SPRING LAMB

Salt and pepper a young leg of lamb, spread it generously with dry mustard and pack it with dark brown sugar as you would a ham for baking. Place uncovered in a preheated 325° oven and watch that the sugar does not scorch on the bottom of the roaster. Baste often with the sharp-sweet juices and if the sugar begins to burn, add a small amount of black coffee. At any rate, when the lamb is about half done, pour over a cup of strong black coffee, left over from breakfast or lunch. Roast until the meat is tender but not dry; about 2 hours should be long enough. Thicken the gravy with cornstarch and melt into it 1 good t of currant jelly. Let the sauce simmer 5 minutes, adding more water if needed.

૨≫ SPINACH AND SOUR CREAM

Wash freshly picked spinach (1 lb. should serve three) and
lift from the water, letting it drain a moment in your hands
before tossing into a large pot. Add no more water, cover, and
place over low heat. Don't cook it too long. If the spinach is
very tender, 5 minutes might be ample time. The leaves
should wilt, but still retain their shape, and this is a reward-
ing change from the baby-food purée into which spinach is
ordinarily humbled. Uncover, turn the heat high, and let all
the remaining water boil away. Chop the spinach coarsely,
just enough so that the leaves are manageable on a fork. Salt,
pepper, dress it lightly with 1 heaping T sour cream per
pound, remove from fire and sprinkle it with a few drops of
lemon juice. Now you will know what an honorable vegetable spinach really is.

૨≫ OVEN-ROASTED NEW POTATOES

Peel and wash as many medium-size new potatoes (not the
very small salad potatoes) as you will need. Cut them into
quarters lengthwise and soak them in cold water for an hour.
Drain and dry. Salt them, be liberal with freshly ground pepper, and pour over them enough melted butter to coat each
one. Place them in a shallow dish in one layer. Toss a little
minced green onion or parsley or chives over them. Bake in
the oven along with the lamb during the last hour until they
are tender and crisp, basting often with the butter and adding more if necessary.

   This dish may be varied by replacing the butter with olive
oil, and sprinkling the potatoes with grated Parmesan cheese
before roasting. Many friends prefer them this way, especially
with the rare roast lamb given below, but I don't.

ಕಿ RARE ROAST LEG OF LAMB

Insert 3 or 4 cloves of garlic into the leg of lamb, and don't use too large a leg. Salt and pepper it, dredge it lightly with flour. Put into a 350° preheated oven. After 20 minutes pour over ½ cup strong black coffee, or ¼ cup coffee and ¼ cup dry red wine, continue basting with this, and hold your breath while I tell you to cook the roast no longer than one hour in all. You won't want gravy to serve with this. Put the leg of lamb on a heated platter, let a few pats of butter melt over it. The butter will blend with the natural juices of the pink, succulent roast as you slice it *as thinly as possible*, and a little of this sauce should be served over each portion. It is amazing how cooking lamb as rare as you would steak or a beef rib roast makes it a wholly different meat than any you have tasted before—and delicious too.

ಕಿ LAMB HASH

If you have been provident enough to cook a sufficient quantity of spinach and potatoes along with either the rare or sugared leg of lamb so that there will be leftovers of all three, a wonderful hash awaits you the next day. Chop them all together, moisten with a little cream or leftover gravy from which the fat has been skimmed, and fry to a crisp undercrust in as much butter as needed. This hash is worth planning ahead for.

And for dessert at the Barkers' dinner party that night Miss Schneider had brought several of the pies for which she is famous. The sight of them soothed even Matt's loneliness and panic. Each year as spring is at its fullest and berries ripen, the faces in Miss Schneider's classroom grow brighter because the children know that one of these days she will bring her special treat to school and serve it to them during afternoon recess. It is a holiday time then. Miss Schneider has taught for nearly forty years; grownups in the village remember this happy moment from their own childhood and tell their children long before they enter Miss Schneider's grade of the treat that will one day come to them. It would be unthinkable for a springtime to pass without that wonderful day when she brings the pie. The children themselves, long ago, named it. Through the years it has never been called anything but Schoolteacher Pie.

৩৯ SCHOOLTEACHER PIE

Hull and halve a dozen large, fresh strawberries when they are at their peak of ripeness, sweet but still firm. Sugar them lightly (I also add a little kirsch) and let them stand. Mix a rich *muerbe teig* of ¼ lb. butter, 1 cup flour, ¼ t salt, 2 T milk and 1 T sugar—it will be crumbly and must be pressed into the bottom and sides of a shallow pan, building the sides about 1¼" high. Bake in a moderate oven until done, about half an hour. Let cool. Drain the strawberries well (drink the drained-off kirsch!) and place the berries in the baked pie crust, pouring over them the following:

Scald 1 pint whipping cream in a double boiler, and add to it ¼ t salt and ¼ cup sugar. In a bowl beat 6 egg yolks until they are creamy and pour the cream over the eggs. Cook in the double boiler until the cream coats a spoon. Remove from heat and add 1 t vanilla. When it begins to cool, pour this mixture over the berries in the pie shell. Chill thoroughly. Shortly before serving sprinkle 1 cup of brown sugar over the top and place under the broiler 5 minutes, or just long enough for the sugar to melt and form a crust. Chill

again. The children love it when Miss Schneider decorates
the pie with two or three large beautiful whole strawberries
with their hulls, placed in a small nest of whipped cream in
the center of the pie.

Driving home sleepily after the Barkers' party, I was glad
I could experience springtime in the country. There have
been many times since when the seasons and a certain dish
merge. Baby chickens are the official fowl of spring and
rightly so when they are served for a first evening meal eaten
outdoors on the dining terrace. On your plate waits a crisp,
delicate broiler. This is the exact moment too, I've learned
at last, for the dandelion and bacon salad. Listen to the phoebe
in the woods and the cowbird on the telephone wire overhead
mocking the phoebe—all sounds fall so pristinely these evenings. Watch the young night touch the hills, and with the
chicken sip a light wine in which for several hours you've
steeped a sprig of woodruff from the woods or herb garden
(this is how May wine gets its flavor).
    Some farmers, though, do not think it economical to kill
their chickens when they are still very small. Sometimes
Ruth and John Hummock across the road will let me have
one, but this is neighborly indulgence. More often I come
away with one of last year's birds weighing nearly four
pounds, but it is still tender, not fatty, and always plucked
and cleaned as no butcher-shop bird has ever been cleaned.
It is perfect to steam with a cream and watercress sauce.
    Ruth and John Hummock have their own rite of spring.
For years they have baffled and annoyed their neighbors by
producing sweet corn several weeks before anyone else's will
ripen. But calling for a chicken one afternoon I caught Ruth
at their trick. On their glassed-in, sunny porch were strips of

sod. John digs them as soon as the ground thaws. They are overturned, early corn is sown in them, and when danger of frost is past the sod is cut into chunks and the seedlings transplanted right in the sod to the garden without harm. It is extra work and worth it when the first longed-for ears ripen.

For me, two more dishes belong to springtime. In the village I will see the first kids racing along the sidewalks on roller skates, their legs still wobbly from winter, the sound of their skates on cement echoing hollowly in the still afternoon —I don't know whether it is a Proustian childhood association or not, but I know it is time to have fried salt pork with creamed new peas and potatoes for supper. The other I hunger for as soon as the first green onions are ready in the garden; they are cooked with pork chops and sour cream.

ಶ SPRING-BROILED CHICKEN

Young chickens are so often maltreated, their flavor hidden under a coat of coarse crumbs, further permeated by cooking oil which tastes as though fish had been fried in it the night before. A 2 or 2½ lb. chicken will taste as delicate as it should if it is halved or disjointed, dusted with salt, fresh pepper, paprika and 1 T minced parsley, and sprinkled lightly with lemon juice. Place skin side up in a shallow pan, dot with ½ stick butter (no substitutes), and broil about ¾ hour or until done with the broiler set at 350° and the door kept closed. The chicken should be in the middle of the oven, not too near the broiler, and turned when it is crisp. Baste often and if the skin seems in danger of becoming too brown, switch the oven from broil to bake. About 10 minutes before it is done, pour over ¾ cup sweet light cream; when done, thicken gravy with cornstarch mixed with ½ cup water. Serve with baby carrots and a dandelion salad.

৯ DANDELION SALAD

Wash, dry, and chill some very young dandelion shoots. These can often be found in Italian vegetable markets in large cities, should your own lawn not supply them. Dice bacon, about 1 strip per serving, and fry crisp, drain and crumble over the greens. Sprinkle with salt, fresh pepper; for enough greens for three or four persons, add ½ t sugar, ½ T lemon juice, ½ T cider vinegar, 3 T warm bacon drippings, and toss. This is also a good dressing for other salad greens, particularly watercress or young raw spinach. The first, tiny, scarce dandelion buds are a great delicacy in this salad; as children we fought over them.

৯ STEAMED CHICKEN WITH CREAM
AND WATERCRESS SAUCE

Skin a 3 or 4 lb. whole chicken but cook the skin along with the chicken to flavor the sauce. Rub the chicken with ½ lemon, salt and pepper, and place it in a Dutch oven with 2 cloves, a celery stalk with its leaves, ½ cup water and ½ cup dry white wine. Cook covered until done, adding more water if needed. There should be at least ½ cup broth left after cooking. Strain this sauce, while the chicken waits on a warm platter. Add 1 cup sweet cream to the sauce and thicken with 2 or 3 egg yolks stirred in one at a time over a low fire. Add 1 t capers, or remove from heat and stir in a few drops of lemon juice.

Have cooked watercress ready, by cleaning and cooking 2 bunches of watercress as you would spinach. Drain it very well, chop fine, and season it with salt, pepper, butter, a few drops of tarragon vinegar and, if you like, a touch of garlic. Heat well and spread this over the steamed chicken. Pour the sauce around the chicken and on the sauce lay triangles of bread fried in butter. For a special party, place a fried chicken liver on each toast triangle.

ẽ❧ SALT PORK WITH CREAMED NEW PEAS AND POTATOES

This is a delicious supper, much neglected, and easy to prepare. Slice as much salt pork as is wanted in ⅜″ slices and soak in milk for an hour. Drain, dry with a towel, dredge with flour, pepper it lightly and fry as you would bacon but more slowly. To serve with this: combine a cup of cooked new peas to every 2 cups of very small new potatoes (boiled and then peeled) in a rich cream sauce. Season with salt and pepper; a little fresh basil or a few celery seeds may be added though neither is necessary—it's the taste of freshness that counts.

ẽ❧ PORK CHOPS AND GREEN ONIONS IN SOUR CREAM

Brown 6 pork chops in an iron skillet. Salt and pepper them and add 1 T paprika. Remove to a casserole (I leave them right in the skillet). Clean a handful of young garden onions but leave part of the green tops on them. Put over the chops and cover with 1 cup sour cream. Bake covered in 300° oven about 40 minutes, until chops are tender. The gravy is delicious over rice. If you prefer, the green onions may be stewed separately in as little water as possible, drained, buttered, and put over the chops before serving.

And I can't let those first tender scallions ripen in the garden without telling what they will do for a humble fried egg sandwich.

⅋ FRIED EGG AND GREEN ONION SANDWICH

Fry a strictly fresh egg slowly, covered, in a good portion of butter. The butter should not brown; the egg white should remain delicate and the yolk runny. Salt and pepper. Remove egg, add more butter to pan if necessary, turn up heat, and fry 2 slices of fresh white bread on one side only until golden. Place the egg on one slice, cover generously with finely chopped green onions. Add a cautious blob (about ½ t) of chili sauce but only if it is homemade. If not, add a drop, no more, of Worcestershire sauce to the shimmering egg yolk. Cover with the second slice of fried bread. This sandwich is earthy and fattening and messy to eat and wonderful. Don't forget to wipe your plate with the crust.

CHAPTER TWO

GREET THE DAWN

It was Rosalie Barker's husband, Matt, who taught me
about breakfast. One spring dawn he took me fishing. The
lake was choppy, but the awakening sky held a pale green
calm and far above us were migrating white herons; they nest
in a great marsh twenty or thirty miles north of here. It was a
phenomenal sight, the slowly flapping, chalk-white bodies
against the silent sky. Then in their wake, as though they
dragged it after them, came an unexpected sky covering, slate-
colored and smoky. Even before the herons were out of sight
a spring storm had begun.

Matt, big and solid, the rain pellets exploding from his
bald head, docked the boat, yanked off the outboard motor
and yelled to race for the car. Our fishing day was ended before we'd even got our lines into the water.

"Tell you what," Matt said, and looked contented. "I was
getting hungry anyway." He glanced at his watch. "Nearly six.
All I had was some eggs before we set out. You come by the
house and I'll fix us a good pan of apple crisp for breakfast.
What you groaning for?"

For me, an ample morning meal was coffee and coffee

and coffee. Breakfast was a meal for which, through the New York years, I had lost all relish. Perhaps never does the city dweller seem so pathetic as when he is eating the meal that should fortify body and soul. Seated usually at a drugstore counter, he is a forgotten and bewildered man, gulping canned juice, then an egg frizzled in grease accompanied by a woeful slice of toast. A soda mint, and off for the day's work.

Matt changed that. By the time we reached Rosalie's still sleeping kitchen the storm had settled to a nourishing rain, and Matt was soon busy popping on the oven of the gas range, paring winter apples with surprising deftness for hands so raw, and rattling bowls and coffeecake pans out of Rosalie's cupboards.

"Always fix my own breakfast," Matt said. "I let Rosalie sleep. She's got her hands full fixing the big meals of the day."

Since he already had a thick slice of ham frying, and coffee boiling on the stove, and a bowl of hard-boiled eggs on the table, I was wondering how much bigger a meal could be when the stair door opened. There stood Rosalie, dressed, hair neatly combed, face fresh, but her eyes still heavy.

"You fooling around again and messing up my whole kitchen?" Rosalie asked.

"Well, dammit, Rosalie!" Matt broke out like a caught child. "A man's got to eat, don't he?"

Rosalie smiled at me. "He's always getting up in the middle of the night and coming down and trying to cook something, and my kitchen looks like a cyclone struck it."

I did notice then that a web of flour and dribbles of butter had somehow settled over sink and stove and tabletop. Apple parings lay curled everywhere.

Matt's guilt still churned inside him. "Rosalie, dammit! I try to see you get your sleep, don't I?"

"Ever hear of a man who has to have banquets for his breakfast—maple dumplings or veal cakes or apple crisp? Can't eat like ordinary people, bacon and eggs," Rosalie said, again with a smile as she took the flour sifter from Matt's hand. "Here. Let me."

Rosalie took over. The fragrances of boiling (not percolating or dripping or filtering) coffee, and the frying ham (Rosalie swiftly turned the flame low—Matt had it scorching over an inferno), and then the sweetly sharp baking apple crisp, soon stirred in me an appetite that had not been awake at this hour for years.

But even so it was a timid stirring, wavering fearfully each time Rosalie opened the oven door, while Matt hovered over her wondering loudly whether, dammit, the thing was ever going to get done. I looked at Matt with some awe. Even for a man this large and sturdy, a steaming rich confection seemed formidable for breakfast.

"Hold your horses," Rosalie soothed him—and then my appetite vanished again as she reached a final time into the oven to take out the spicy, tart apples with their crust of brown buttery crumbs. Matt followed it to the table like a magnet, bearing in his hands a full pitcher of heavy cream. At suppertime I could have been happy. But for breakfast I could only look at Rosalie stuporously.

"There you are," she said cheerfully.

There we were. And there was pride and expectancy in Rosalie's voice. In the country you might insult your neighbor, or even his wife, but not his wife's cooking. Matt was swinging into his chair as happily as a boy. He cast a side glance at my reluctance. The rain had lifted and the morning sun shot through the window—it was still barely seven. The world was clean and birds shook themselves dry in Rosalie's crab apple tree with its shower of bloom and a spring breeze blew and the kitchen was bright as a new beginning in life, and this moment, in this place, I reflected, should be one of joy.

"Come on eat, man," Matt commanded happily. "Where's your appetite?"

Hesitantly I tasted a forkful of the ham and then the cream-drenched, crusted apples Rosalie had heaped on my plate. It was all wonderful.

୫ APPLE CRISP AND CREAM

Pare half a dozen tart, firm apples and cut each into 8 parts, removing core and seeds. Place the segments closely together in a buttered 8"x12" pan. Mix together 2 T granulated sugar and ¼ t cinnamon and sprinkle this over the apples. Now mix 1 cup flour with ¼ cup brown sugar, and rub into it with the fingertips ½ cup butter until it is of a crumbly consistency. Spread this over the apples and pat firm. Bake in 450° oven for ½ hour or until the apples are tender. Eaten warm, either plain or with heavy cream, this is perfect with ham or sausages for breakfast. With hard sauce or sweetened whipped cream it becomes dessert.

With the apple crisp and ham that morning I first tasted country-boiled coffee and, the wise words of coffee experts and manufacturers of dripolators, percolators and filter machines notwithstanding, this to me has been the only real coffee ever since. I don't even mind the occasional grounds that escape through the strainer. This *tastes* like coffee and not the least of the enjoyment of it is the aroma while the pot is boiling. Rosalie used an old enamel pot and I scoured the countryside until I found one like it. It has become revered.

ໞ THE RIGHT WAY TO MAKE COFFEE—BOILED

Into a very clean, fresh pot put a rounded T of good coffee (and I've learned that the more expensive brands are not always the best) for each cup of cold water. Good water, such as we have in the country, is of real importance and, if necessary, even bottled spring water should not be thought an extravagance. Put on a very low flame. Increase the heat as the water warms, and when it has reached a gently rolling boil, let it cook for 5 minutes more. Take from the heat, add ½ cup cold water, and let it rest a minute for the grounds to settle. This is coffee.

Country breakfasts are of necessity ample, for a furrow can be ploughed straighter on a full stomach. Also, in the country, there is more time to enjoy them. A tractor waiting in the shed won't take off on the dot like a suburban train. On the breakfast tables of my neighbors are bowls of berries, pitchers of milk and cream, platters of sausage and eggs, hot cereal, toast and biscuits, with the women comfortable about the sink or stove, the radio playing, the men still stretching and in no hurry to reach field or village, and the children finding time between gulps to rush out to the barn to see the new kittens. There is always a third cup of coffee and with it, of course, more food must be consumed, slowly, enjoyably, while the May sun lifts the chill from the earth outside.

At Rosalie's house breakfasts are always as hearty as lunch. From her I learned many filling dishes, all of which Matt wolfs with delight at the crack of dawn: tender veal cakes, spicy and crisp, or eggs poached in cream with small croquettes of leftover veal, or a baked ham and apple roll. All of these are delicious for a company or late, leisurely Sunday breakfast out on the terrace, while the chipmunks come begging for nuts and the Chicago-to-Minneapolis planes flash silver in the spring sky above. Since, unlike Rosalie, I do not enjoy leaping from bed to the range, it was a relief to learn that these dishes can be prepared in part the night before.

৪ৢ VEAL CAKES

Cut ½ lb. stewing veal into small pieces and simmer in 4 cups of water until it is tender, about an hour. Remove the meat and put through a food grinder, along with 2 onions. Reduce the broth to 3 cups and add to it 1½ cups stewed tomatoes rubbed through a sieve and 2 t salt. When it is boiling again stir in the meat mixture, pepper to taste, 1 cup cornmeal and, if you like, a dash of chili powder. Cook for half an hour, stirring so that it will not stick. Pour into a greased loaf mold and chill overnight. In the morning slice it and fry in hot oil or fat. With the cakes, serve moist, lightly scrambled eggs.

৪ৢ PANHAS

For this meat cake (where its name comes from I don't know, nor does Rosalie) cook together ½ lb. beef and ½ lb. fat pork in enough water to cover it. When it is soft, put it through a meat grinder. Return the meat to the broth, season with salt, freshly ground pepper and about ½ t each of ground cloves and allspice. Then add buckwheat flour gradually until the mixture is very stiff and separates from the kettle. Put into a buttered loaf pan, chill it, and in the morning fry 1″ slices of these savory cakes in hot fat until the crusts are crisp.

৪ৢ BAKED HAM AND APPLE ROLL

Remove the bone from a large slice of ham no thicker than ¼″. Spread the ham with ½ t dry mustard and 1 t wine vin-

egar mixed together. Slice a tart apple, peeled and cored, as
thinly as possible and lay the slices over the ham in a thin
layer. Sprinkle ¼ cup brown sugar over the apples and roll
up the ham, beginning with the fat side. Skewer the roll together, or tie it with string, place in a buttered pan and brush
butter over the roll. Bake in a 350° oven until the ham and
apples are tender, basting often with orange or any other
fruit juice. This, with waffles or pancakes, makes a memorable
breakfast. For a luncheon dish I use wine for the basting, and
serve it with candied sweet potatoes and a salad.

৪ VEAL CROQUETTES

To a cupful of ground leftover veal (grind along a few raw
mushrooms if you have them) add 2 T butter, a minced
green onion with its greens, a little parsley and 1 t fresh basil
or ½ t dried, and a few leaves of finely chopped fresh spinach or sorrel. Add salt and white pepper. Shape the mixture
into croquettes no larger than walnuts, adding a few drops of
cream if the paste needs moistening, and fry these lightly in
butter. Over them pour a cream sauce, sprinkle with fresh
parsley, chives, chervil or rosemary, and serve with sautéed
mushrooms or scrambled eggs, or

৪ EGGS POACHED IN CREAM

Into a small saucepan put ½ cup or more light cream and
1 T butter and bring to a rapid boil. Slip in the eggs, one at
a time, turn the heat low, cover, and cook slowly for 4 minutes. With the eggs served right in the cream, this is a really
delicious dish.

But it was maple dumplings, and Matt Barker's passion
for them, that nearly destroyed my growing respect for break-

fast as an enjoyable meal. Among my hills is a small stand of sugar maples, the only ones in the neighborhood. Matt worked up to tapping them slyly and deviously.

"Like trees?" he asked, driving up one year just at the first glimmer of spring.

"Sure I like trees. What are the pails for?"

"Nothing." Matt shrugged. "Just happened to have 'em with me."

"Well, what's this about whether I like trees or not?"

"Thought we just might go take a look at some of yours, that's all."

Matt has known all my trees since he was a boy. He knows which of the hickories and butternuts and black walnuts are likely to produce the best crops, and which of the oaks along the drive is the oldest and which elm was struck by lightning in what year. That morning, the small buckets clanking in his hands, he led me straight to the stand of maples, though until then I did not even know I owned any. There were lingering patches of snow underfoot but the air was warm. Talking about anything under the sun but trees, Matt had tapped the old maples before I knew it, inserted the spigots, and hung up the buckets to catch the run of rising sap.

"Thought you'd like to see how it works. Enjoy showing greenhorns how I tap my sap," he said then. It was already *his* sap. "Once Rosalie gets this sap boiled down, you come over for breakfast some morning and I'll have her fix some maple dumplings."

"Maple *dumplings?*"

"Best food you ever ate."

It hardly seemed a palatable dish but Matt was right: Rosalie "syrups down" as Matt's mother taught her, tossing

thick pork rinds into the bubbling liquid, presumably to keep
the sap from boiling over. All the neighboring children love
this preserved sugary rind. And once they are seen nibbling
away along the streets, their parents know Rosalie's syrup is
done and await her annual summons to a springtime Sunday
pre-church breakfast of maple dumplings and bacon or ham.

ह‍ MAPLE DUMPLINGS

When you first brood about these, your stomach (like mine)
may go queasy; but if you like waffles or pancakes with syrup
you will like these. Sift together 1 cup sifted flour, 1½ t baking powder and ½ t salt, and blend into this mixture 2 T
butter. Gradually add ⅓ cup milk. In a kettle with a tightly
fitting lid bring 1 cup real maple syrup, ½ cup water and 1 T
butter to a boil. Drop the dough into the kettle by small
spoonfuls, cover tightly, and cook *gently* for 15 minutes.
Serve with additional melted butter, syrup, confectioners'
sugar, or tart jam.

Once Matt had awakened my morning appetite I began
to hunger for half-remembered foods: a whiff of blowing lilac
one morning made me start from sleep, ravenous for pancakes
the way my Aunt Ida used to make them, bubbly yet crisp. In
the same instant I recalled how we used to visit her each May
of my youth and how a bower of lilacs grew under her kitchen
windows. That morning, in my mother's frayed cookbook, I
found her sister's recipe, waiting all this while, along with the
Easter Morning Eggs my mother used to have ready for us
each year after we had ransacked the house to find our Easter
nests. And the creamy Goldenrod Eggs we loved as children.

All of these, I have discovered with pleasure, taste as good now as they did then.

From friends and neighbors have come other breakfast recipes out of their own memories, all a welcome change from the routine juice, eggs and toast. A visiting Southerner taught me about his family's white spoon bread and chicken hash as well as about a sizzling shrimp omelet: sometimes both appeared on the table together for an illustrious guest. From a Finnish friend I learned about thin, delicate pancakes no larger than a silver dollar, drenched in butter and dotted with wild blackberry jam. At the great summer home of Mrs. Brubaker, a neighbor on one of the many nearby lakes, I tasted rolled, filled French pancakes, topped with sour cream, made by her chef Eugene as they have always been made in his native Belgium. A visitor from Maine late one Sunday morning supplied a cheese pudding with a succulent dried beef sauce faintly redolent of curry powder—the only time I've tasted dried beef worth its salt.

Sometimes now, out here, we will even rise in the cool breezes of a spring dawn, needing no further goading than the prospect of Aunt Ida's egg pancakes or Rosalie's veal cakes. Or a party has lasted too long, and hash made from last night's roast or fowl seems the perfect greeting to the rising sun, before we separate for sleep. Taken before or after sleeping, it is a happy thing, a friend has said, that breakfasts were designed for the morning hours. Then musically the birds are at their noisiest and boldest, like brash, young composers. Trees and hills glisten. And after a walk down the meadow and back with a stop to pick a few wild shooting stars or to watch an equally watchful possum, now that I am used to country ways my appetite is ravenous.

ぷ AUNT IDA'S EGG PANCAKES

Mix together 1 cup flour, ½ t salt and 1½ t baking powder.
Stir into it 1 cup milk, or enough to make the batter runny,
then 2 beaten egg yolks and 2 T melted ham fat, if possible, or butter. Separately beat 2 egg whites until stiff and
fold them into the batter with as little commotion as possible. Don't beat after adding the whites. Drop by large spoonfuls into a generous amount of hot fat, turn when they are
bubbly, and fry golden. Again, if possible, use ham fat for the
frying (for its pure, delicate flavor).

ぷ FINNISH PANCAKES

Beat 4 eggs well and to them add 1 cup sugar, ½ t salt,
4 cups milk and 2 T melted butter. Mix well and pour over
2 cups flour and beat the batter until it is absolutely lump-
less. The batter is improved if it is left to stand an hour
or two before it is used. For the frying, only melted butter
should be used. These pancakes may be fried either in a
standard Finnish pancake mold or dropped in very small
amounts on an ordinary griddle; they should be no larger
than 3″ across, almost paper-thin, and fried only to a gentle
gold. Serve 6 in a stack for each person, in a pool of more
melted butter. With these, serve side dishes of fresh blackberries, black currants, or blueberries, stewed in sugar and
chilled, or wild blackberry jam. My Finnish friend and I have
often enjoyed these small marvels as a closing midnight tribute to an evening of talk and bourbon.

ぷ FILLED FRENCH PANCAKES

Beat 6 eggs well, then add 6 T flour and again beat well. Add
1 t salt and 2 cups milk and stir until smooth. Into a hot
pan of butter pour enough batter to make a large thin pan-

cake. Cover the pan while cooking, and turn once. The pancake, when lightly browned on each side, should be filled as follows:

Mix together ½ lb. strained cottage cheese, 3 t sugar, the grated rind of 1 lemon and 1 whole egg. Spread some of this on each pancake, roll, place on a warm platter and keep hot in a warm oven. Just before serving, top each pancake with sour cream and garnish the platter with chicken livers fried in butter and parsley or browned pork links.

ࢻ CHICKEN HASH WITH SPOON BREAD

This is for a gala breakfast or even luncheon. Melt 2 T chicken fat (or, if need be, butter) in a saucepan, blend in 1½ T flour, and gradually add 1 cup rich chicken stock. When it begins to boil add 2 cups finely minced cooked chicken; the meat should be chopped to the size of small peas. Remove from heat, season moderately, and add 1 T chopped pimento, 1 T either chopped mushrooms or green olives and a little parsley, but nothing more, for the joy of this hash is its unadulterated chicken flavor. Place it in a buttered casserole and bake at 350° for about 20 minutes. Serve these delicate nuggets with a white spoon bread, the recipe for which is given on page 89.

ࢻ BAKED EGGS ON TOAST WITH HASH

Make 2 cups of cream sauce and flavor it well with salt, pepper, and a few herbs such as basil, chives or parsley. Reserve half the sauce; to the remainder add a jigger of sherry, 1 T chopped green pepper, and ½ cup or slightly more of finely chopped leftover lamb, veal or fowl. Simmer a minute or two, stirring carefully, to let the flavors blend.

Toast 4 slices of stale bread, butter them lightly, and put

them into a shallow baking dish. Pour the reserved plain sauce over the toast. On this, break 4 eggs carefully so that they will remain whole, and then gently pour over them the creamed hash. Bake in a 400° oven until the eggs are set, being careful not to let the yolks harden (5 or 6 minutes should do it). Now hurry it to the table. Sometimes I think this is the best of all Sunday noon breakfast dishes, unless it be

ᘒ SHRIMP OMELET AU GRATIN

Have ready and keep warm 2 cups of light cream sauce into which you have broken up about a dozen cooked shrimps. Add to it 1 t capers, salt and pepper, and, if you like, a few chopped fresh fennel fronds or a pinch of caraway. Butter well a shallow but large baking dish, heat it in a 400° oven, and into it pour 3 eggs beaten frothy with 2 T light cream. Bake 10 minutes, or until the omelet is puffed and cooked. Pour the creamed shrimps over it, sprinkle with Parmesan cheese and buttered bread crumbs and place under the broiler until it is bubbly and browned. Instead of shrimps, cooked lobster pieces, crabmeat, small fish balls or slivers of chicken breast may be used—all are excellent.

ᘒ CHEESE PUDDING AND DRIED BEEF SAUCE

This too makes an impressive dish for a company breakfast. For the pudding, butter generously 5 slices of bread and cut into cubes. Mix together 3 beaten egg yolks, 1 cup milk, a pinch of salt, ½ t wet mustard and ½ lb. grated sharp cheddar cheese, and fold in 3 egg whites beaten stiff. Pour this over the bread cubes in a deep buttered casserole, mix and bake in a 375° oven for ¾ hour or until puffed and brown. It should have a nice crust.

While it is baking, melt 1 bouillon cube in 2 large T butter, add 2 T flour and stir in ¾ cup milk and ¾ cup cream or condensed milk. Toss in 3 chopped scallions when the sauce has thickened. Next ½ t dry mustard, salt, pepper, 2 hard-boiled eggs chopped fine, ½ t curry powder or more to taste, and lastly a 2½ oz. jar of dried beef which has been rinsed well to extract the salt, squeezed dry and then shredded. Serve this sauce over whopping spoonfuls of the crusty, fragrant pudding.

ã GOLDENROD EGGS

Melt 2 T butter and stir into it 1 T flour. When it bubbles, gradually stir in ¾ cup milk and a few T cream and stir until thick. Add ½ t salt and ¼ t white pepper, 2 T grated Swiss cheese, then the whites of 4 hard-boiled eggs well chopped. Cook for a minute longer and pour over rounds of buttered toast on which have been placed ¼″ rounds of grilled ham. Have ready the yolks of 4 hard-boiled eggs, rubbed through a sieve, and sprinkle these over the tops.

ã EASTER MORNING EGGS

These should greet every child on Easter morn. Separate the whites and yolks of 6 hard-boiled eggs and cut the whites into long thin strips. Set these aside in a warm oven and butter them now and then to keep from drying, while you mix with the yolks 1 cup of finely ground cooked chicken or ham (use canned deviled ham if you wish), 1 t chopped parsley, salt and pepper, and cream or butter to moisten. Shape this mixture into balls the size of a robin's eggs, heap on a festive dish, and arrange the whites around them like a nest. Around all pour 1 cup hot cream sauce.

Each Easter morning this waited on our breakfast table, the tiny golden eggs in their nest of pure white on an emer-

ald lawn of parsley over which paraded yellow marshmallow
chicks to be gobbled for dessert by my sister, cousins and me.
I still enjoy it as much today—without the marshmallow
chicks, however.

CHAPTER THREE

FISHING WEATHER

THAT FIRST MORNING when Matt took me fishing, even though we caught no fish, another memory returned and with it tastes I thought I had forgotten. They must have been reborn by sight of the bulrushes rimming the lake, the calls of the herons overhead, the surprising gentleness of the spray, and the glimpse of a dead tamarack swamp in a hidden bay, the gaunt drowned trees standing there like ghosts of themselves. I had not seen these sights since I was a boy.

As music is to some men, and gambling to others, fishing (and eating the fish) was to my father. He had been born on his father's farm not far from where I live now; often, while I was young, we returned there from town to visit. Each spring now when I wake to a warm cloudy day and catch the beckoning breeze, I can hear him again, his voice, laughing with hope, rising clearly through the heat register in my grandmother's kitchen up to the cold bedroom where I lay. "By God, Ma," he is saying to my patient mother, "what a day to go fishing! Smell that air? Hear how still it is? They'll bite like suckers today."

Fishing weather had caught him. I knew his line well.

My mother did not like fishing, but without her he could not go, since these were family vacations. But his persuasion never failed on her quiet geniality and within the hour we were off in his touring car for one of the nearby lakes, a large basket of food supplies on the rear seat beside me—even a home-stuffed sausage, should my father's great fish not oblige him by being hooked.

The first glimpse of water made him snort. "Look at that, will you, Ma! There's some big babies waiting in there! You sure you brought plenty good butter along? And the frying pan?"

He was a young, lean man then, jumping from the car. I don't know which he enjoyed most, the anticipation of catching the fish or eating them after my mother had prepared them in any of the half a dozen ways she had learned from her German-born mother. Soon my father and I were in a boat while my mother watched after us, resting on the running board of the car. The sky mercifully had held its cloud cover, the air was still and mild. Bulrushes rimmed the shore; in a hidden bay we rowed past a dead tamarack swamp; dark green weeds trailed after the boat and spray splashed on us from the oars with surprising gentleness and overhead migrating birds called.

We drifted near the edge of the rushes. Suddenly there was the *whir-r-r* of the reel as he cast out true and straight, a tremendous distance. Then the plop of the minnow as it struck the water, the soft mist spewing from his line as he reeled in evenly, the awful silence and waiting, then suddenly —the lunge at the end of the line, his rod bending perilously, the rushes quivering as the snared pickerel or pike sought shelter.

And all the while my father fought and maneuvered, his

face alive and strong. The fish splashed, then wallowed near the surface playing dead in exhaustion, then dived straight downward like a rock. While the line shivered taut and sometimes went horrifyingly slack but then tightened again like a cable, my father never stopped crooning: "C'mon baby, come to papa! See him, boy? See what a beauty he is! C'mon, c'mon, baby. *Papa catch you like a man, Mama fry you in the pan!*"

And indeed, waiting back on shore, my mother had her frying pan ready. Then, under the softly leafing trees beside the calm lake, came one of the best meals I can remember.

৪৯ PAN-FRIED FISH

While my father whistled and cleaned the fish, sending up an opalescent shower of scales, I built a fire. Pickerel or pike or bass were cut into large pieces, or fillets, but not boned, while perch or blue gills were left whole. With deft hands my mother dusted the fish with flour (cornmeal was never used as it toughens tender skin!), salted it, peppered it generously, and into a lake of hot fresh butter in the sizzling pan it went, lots of butter, and nothing but butter. It needed only 8 or 10 minutes of frying, my mother turning it often, releasing marvelous aromas from the pan, and when it was lightly, crisply browned on all sides it was done. It was not drained on paper as cooks do nowadays, but the golden butter was allowed to ooze onto our plates. We ate the white-flaked fish with firm bread and more butter and homemade dill pickles. My mother always gave me the delicate tail end of the fish to eat, promising with certainty it would teach me how to dance.

After that rainy morning on the lake with Matt Barker, I recollected other more elaborate ways in which my mother used to prepare fish, in the spacious, warm convenience of her own kitchen. From a week's stay at my grandfather's we would return with a packing crate of fish, carefully swathed in wet pickerel weed and cradled between huge chunks of ice. We gave fish to our uncles and aunts and cousins; we gave fish to our neighbors, for there were no deep freezers then to store them. And for another week we ate black bass and northern pike and glisteny pickerel—baked, floating in a pool of stewed tomatoes and celery and spices; or stuffed with raisins, which was a filling usually reserved for black bass though I've since found it delicious for any fish large enough to be stuffed, especially red snapper or whitefish. Some of the pickerel was always pickled, the crammed, watery-colored Mason jars stored away to be opened for Sunday suppers or midnight lunch.

Best of all, however, was the fish soup my mother made, always served with a towering heap of mashed potatoes as well as an extra platter of fish fried in flour and butter as she fried them on the lake shore. I have introduced Matt to fish soup. He agrees huskily that there is nothing so fine on a mild spring day, when the fishing has been good and the twilight sun breaks through the benign clouds as you sit at table peaceably tired after a day on the water. Quarts of beer are consumed along with the creamy, silvery soup before you know it.

২৯ FISH SOUP

Any large fish may be used and if desired it may be boned before serving; around our supper table, however, the careful scrutiny for the tiny sharp bones was always part of the excitement. (And if you swallow one, quickly cram down a slice of soft bread!) Cut the fish into large pieces and pour over it almost to cover a liquor made as follows: half water,

half *white* vinegar, 1 or 2 sliced onions, 1 stalk of celery and
its leaves cut up, several coarsely chopped sprigs of parsley,
1 t pickling spices, ½ t each whole peppercorns and whole
allspice, and 2 bay leaves. Sometimes I also add ½ cup dry
white wine. Boil the fish in the liquor until the flesh flakes
away from the bones easily with a fork (but the flesh should
still be firm), remove the fish and reduce the liquor to one
half. Meanwhile beat well 1 whole egg, add to it ½ pt. light
cream, beat again and stir this into the liquor, beating all the
while. Return the fish to the soup, add finely chopped parsley, and heat only. This soup should not be served in a bowl
but on a plate, ladled generously over a heap of mashed
potatoes, whipped sheer as a cloud but yet not so moist that
the soup will make them soppy. And pass around an extra
platter of pan-fried fish, either reserved portions of the fish
used for the soup, or perch fillets.

ࣝ BAKED STUFFED PIKE

My mother always favored pike for this dish, though whitefish or any other large fish is good. Keep the fish whole, bone
it, and lay it in a shallow, attractive pan. Rub the fish well
with lemon, salt and fresh pepper. Into the cavity, stuff 2
well chopped onions, 2 or 3 chopped stalks of celery and
leaves and some chopped chives. Season it all again, add a
dozen whole allspice and 2 crumbled bay leaves and pour over
1 can stewed tomatoes. Top with generous pieces of butter
and bake in a moderate oven for 40 minutes or until done.
Sprinkle it well with buttered bread crumbs and run under
the broiler for a moment. Serve right in the pan.

ࣝ RAISIN STUFFING FOR BASS

This is also good for pike, red snapper or whitefish. Dress the
fish whole. For a 4 or 5 lb. fish, cook 1 large chopped onion

and ½ cup chopped celery slowly in 4 T butter until tender but do not let it brown. Add salt, pepper, and a large pinch of powdered thyme or 1 t fresh thyme. Pour this over 3 cups of bread, softened in milk or dry white wine and squeezed dry. Add to this ⅓ cup seedless raisins, mix, and pack gently into the fish. Bake for 10 minutes at 500° in a buttered shallow pan, then reduce heat to 400° and bake about 40 minutes longer. Serve with tartar sauce.

❧ PICKLED PICKEREL

A pickerel is preferred for this, though pike or crappies may also be used. Cut the fish into small fillets, cover with water and add 2 onions cut in rings, 1 t whole black pepper and another of whole allspice, 1 T sugar or more to taste, and ½ lemon cut in slices. Boil all together until the fish is nearly done and add white vinegar to equal the amount of liquid left over the fish. Boil until done. Add 1 T capers and seal in glass jars. When we had them, my mother always tossed ½ cup hickory nut meats into the pickling liquid. With nuts or without, one jar of the herring was always reserved to be eaten by us, for good luck, on the stroke of twelve on New Year's Eve, along with a bowl of homemade pickled beets dressed with sour cream.

With our fried or baked fish dinners at home, cucumbers were always served, either sweet-sour in vinegar or bathed in sweet cream (my favorite); also, boiled potatoes in sour cream. Over the years I have found no reason to alter these perfect foils.

❧ CUCUMBERS IN CREAM

Pare 2 cucumbers and slice them as thin as possible. Soak for 1 hour in salt water and then squeeze them as dry as possible with your hands. Mix together ¼ cup sugar, ¼ cup white vinegar, and ¾ cup sweet light cream. Let the cucumbers soak in this another hour and serve in sauce dishes. No other seasonings should be added, neither salt nor pepper, and the cucumbers should never go near a refrigerator: all the soaking should be done at room temperature, even on a hot day. The aroma is irresistible as you pass by them, so dip in for a sample while you wait, as we always did, which is why 2 cucumbers are needed. These are also excellent with roast pork.

੨∾ SWEET-SOUR CUCUMBER AND ONION
Prepare 1 large cucumber by paring and slicing as above, and after it has been soaked in salt water and drained, mix it with 1 Bermuda onion sliced into thin rings. Salt, fresh pepper, ½ cup sugar dissolved in ½ cup white vinegar, some chopped parsley, and the whole left to marinate for ½ hour, make this a delicious salad to accompany fish of any sort.

੨∾ BOILED POTATOES IN SOUR CREAM
Pare 4 medium potatoes, cut into quarters, and place in a saucepan along with 1 small minced onion, salt and pepper, and water to cover. Simmer only until tender. Drain well, add 2 T butter and 4 T sour cream, cover the pan and shake gently.

And any fish, small pan-fried perch or magnificently garnished lake trout, will taste better if it is accompanied by fried corn cakes. I was first served these by a Southern friend and I can't imagine why we in other parts in the country pay so little attention to them.

৯৶ FRIED CORN CAKES

Mix together 2 cups cornmeal, preferably the white and waterground, ½ t baking soda, 1 t salt, 1 t baking powder, and 1 T flour. Add 2 or 3 T chopped onion, then stir in 1 cup buttermilk, and lastly 1 whole egg beaten. Have a frying pan ready with a generous supply of hot lard or cooking oil and drop in the batter by spoonfuls; make the cakes thin and delicate for the dinner table, larger and huskier for an outdoor fish fry. Fry golden brown and drain on paper.

One other recipe must be added, lest anyone be lucky enough some spring day to happen by accident upon its lovely ingredients, as I did in our village one day. It startled me to find a large, hastily scrawled placard in the village market advertising FRESH SMETLES. HURRY! SPECIAL!

"What's so special? What's a smetle?" I asked our butcher.

"Smelts. *Smelts*. Can't you read?" he asked, and pointed to a huge barrel full of tiny glistening fish, some three, some six inches long. "Fresh smelts. Little fishes. The run started last night."

Smelts, I was told then, are small, troutlike fish that begin their run to spawn in early spring—torrents of them, jamming the creeks, rivers and lakes. "You can walk on 'em," John, the butcher, said. "You catch 'em with a butterfly net —best way to scoop 'em up. Handy to have a baby buggy along too. Easiest way to haul 'em home."

The run lasts only a few days. Then the wonder dies. You can't taste them again for another year. They can usually be found for two or three days during spring in large city markets, though now sometimes they can also be found frozen. Grab them up. John told me how to prepare them.

ஐ FRIED SMELTS

Cut off the heads and tails, draw them and wipe them with a clean cloth but do not wash the smelts. Dredge them with flour. Fill a pan half full of lard and have it boiling when the smelts are dropped in so that they float; without a sufficient quantity of boiling lard the fish will sink and become dark and greasy. Fry about 10 minutes and drain on paper. They should be crunchy, yet sweet and tender. Sprinkle them with chives or parsley and lemon juice; serve them, steaming and fragrant on a bed of watercress, with boiled new potatoes left in their skins.

Some people, John says, prefer not to eviscerate them and also leave on the heads and tails. "Makes 'em more crackly." But I don't know.

CHAPTER FOUR

THE RICH LADY

BUT THE COUNTRYSIDE here is not all sleepy village and farm and hidden lakes for a fisherman to wait out the dawn. There are the lovely old remodeled houses, and some strikingly new, of city workers who prefer country air and country habits for their children and themselves.

Each morning and evening a stream of commuters' cars files by on the main highway and no one minds or regrets the hour's drive into town and back to earn the livelihood that makes the country house possible. Even on blizzardy days newcomers soon develop remarkable hardiness: the warning howl of wind that can panic you in town is a comforting sigh out here, a promise of a dawdling dinner once safely home and then a long night's sound sleep. What's more, there's an excuse for not getting into the office next morning. Even the grueling snow-shoveling session has its rewards. A neighbor will stop by to help, soon you share a cup of hot coffee, sweetened with a slug of Irish whisky.

Beside these commuters' acres pocketed between village and farm, there are the "summer" lakes. From an observation

46

tower nearby you can count twenty-eight of them and by June's end the imposing houses that rim them will be cheerfully crowded with their city owners and their procession of lightly clad guests. Each year, by mid-May, I find myself waiting for signs of life in one of them particularly.

It is really not yet summer as I drive past the lakes expectantly, for the slim black locusts in the woods still hold their fronds of sweet blossom and the wild crab apples have only begun to shed their pink flowers, and sometimes gusts of wind still rise from over the hills, reminding me that winter is not as far past as I thought. Around the lakes the spacious houses still stand shuttered and dark and lonely; only occasional glimpses of awakening life are seen—a gardener spading the flower beds, a screened porch being painted, a sailboat being hauled from a boathouse.

But then the news I have been waiting for spreads like the pollen of the blooming trees: the rich lady has moved out to the country. She can never wait. Her house a mile away from mine is being opened and overnight it will explode into life and fun. An army of gardeners is rolling her lawns, a call goes through the countryside for extra help during the summer, kitchenmaids, parlormaids, houseboys, and the big pier is being repaired after the damage of winter. Sailboats will hover like water bugs against its pilings all through the next three months. The porches and old-fashioned teahouse and new guesthouse will be crowded with guests and there will be lawn parties and one big fete on the Fourth of July with platforms erected over the tennis court and people dancing under the hot moon. Right now, however, evenings are still chilly. But that does not stop Mrs. Brubaker from moving to the country, even though her huge house has no furnace and is still damp from its winter dormancy. Instead, fires roar in a dozen fireplaces, burning in a week end the wood supply that would last me a winter.

Mrs. Brubaker is one of the nicest women I have ever known. She is warm, gracious, shrewd, dignified. She winters in Colorado because her chef is asthmatic and requires the altitude; but before the end of May they are all back—including Eugene, the Belgian chef, who, I am grateful, is not stingy with his recipes.

Mrs. Brubaker and Eugene and I had a conference in her kitchen one day; my affection for her became lasting when she told with laughter of her first experience in running a household, long ago when she was a bride. Her new cook asked for bay leaves and dutifully Mrs. Brubaker ordered them from her grocer—a dollar's worth she thought would do. The grocer rode along in the wagon with the delivery boy to see for himself just exactly how his new client was planning to use a bushel basketful.

I hadn't known that households such as hers still exist. Her house, with its pillars and porticoes, is roughly the size and design of the Museum of Natural History in New York; each summer she still entertains here as handsomely as she did fifty years ago. She loves this countryside—its hills, lakes, the wildflowers, the hardwoods, her neighbors, social and rural alike—and she thrives on her luncheons and dances where she maneuvers like a general.

However, one year, she caught the less formal spirit of the younger summer crowd around her (who are not even remotely as rich as she is and sometimes give parties to which to her calm amusement the guests come dressed like hayseeds) and decided with considerable ebullience to entertain at a rustic luncheon (the invitations said), at which fifty of us sat down in her marble sunroom to a lunch of hamburgers on buns passed by a dozen servants on the largest silver trays I have ever seen. Champagne too. I think she was not wholly convinced by her own innovation, though, for waiting discreetly on buffet tables in the corners were mounds of lobster salad. The salad was never mentioned or passed. It was just there in case someone needed it.

She has also commented with bright frankness as shad roe canapés were being handed around on her terrace during cocktails, "I like fancy foods better than plain cooking, don't you?"

Her food is always fancy and delicious. On a Sunday I have lunched at her home on mushrooms for which a hefty sirloin steak had been utilized only for the preparation of the accompanying sauce and then discarded, and well worth it.

ε℘ MUSHROOMS IN BEEF SAUCE ON TOAST

Brace yourself to use a pound of beefsteak for each pound of mushrooms. Soak the mushrooms 5 or 10 minutes in salt water, drain, wipe dry, and sauté in 4 T butter for about 3 minutes. Salt, pepper, remove from fire and keep warm. Trim nearly all the fat from the steak and grind it raw, hoarding any juices that drip out. Melt butter in another skillet, add the steak, brown it gently, add salt, a pinch of cayenne, ½ cup hot water, a jigger of Madeira and ½ cup champagne (best champagne, Eugene says). Fry the meat until all the juices can be extracted from it by pressing it with the back of a large wooden spoon. He can accomplish this merely by tipping the pan but I have found it more practical, if less flashy, to put the mixture in a sieve and squeeze the juices back into a skillet with a spoon.

The dead steak you throw away, Eugene grins. But that I doubt. Mrs. Brubaker owns a well-fed schnauzer. Nevertheless, the steak never appears in this dish again. (I save it for

meat loaf or croquettes.) Only the rich juice is used, reduced slightly, and then added to the mushrooms. Toss the
mushrooms about in the juice over a medium flame until
they are just tender—about 2 minutes. Serve with broiled
ham on thin toast made of the highest quality bread. If it is
possible to toast the bread before an open fire, the result is
even better.

Mrs. Brubaker allows Eugene to prepare all the menus.
Besides sharing his recipes with me, he has taught me four of
the invaluable secrets of his profession. (1) How to peel a
hard-boiled egg: crack it mercilessly until it looks as wrinkled
as a shrunken head and the shell will come off in one piece.
(2) How to open a bottle of capers: drop it head down on
the floor. (3) All about the soul of parsley: I didn't quite
catch this—something about it should never be chopped but
left in bouquets. (4) And why it's hopeless for Americans to
try to bake a real French bread, crusty on the outside, tender
and air-pocketed on the inside: no brick ovens.

Mrs. Brubaker knows what she is about in letting Eugene
plan her menus. One starlit June evening he served for a small
dinner party: Pâté Hermitage, Mushroom Salad, Broiled
Squab with Oysters, Pears Eugene. Each was served as a separate course, and a soft wind blew through the high dining
room windows and lifted the curtains to show the stars and
make the candles blink like reflections. The wines were very
light.

ಶಿ PÂTÉ HERMITAGE

The name of Mrs. Brubaker's house is The Hermitage. This
pâté is a variation of Eugene's native Brussels pâté and the
ingredients needed are: 1 medium chicken, 1 lb. calves'

liver, 1¼ lb. bacon, 1 lb. lean pork, 1 cup chopped ham, 6 chicken livers, 2 oz. brandy, salt, bay leaves, thyme, cloves, etc.

Bone the uncooked chicken, reserve the breast, and grind the remaining chicken, including giblets, along with the calves' liver, pork, and 1 lb. of the bacon. Add salt and pepper generously, a little ground cloves, the brandy, and put it all through the grinder again until you have a smooth paste. An earthenware dish with a lid is best for cooking the pâté, though a loaf mold may be used. Line the bottom and sides of the dish with strips of bacon, and place 2 bay leaves and a few leaves of fresh thyme on the bacon. Press half the paste firmly on top of this. Slice the chicken breast, wrap it in thin slices of bacon, and place this on the paste. Next add the chicken livers, previously fried in butter, and then the chopped ham. Cover with the remaining paste, and pack it down as firmly as possible. Cover with more bacon. Put on the lid or cover with wax paper. Put in a pan of water and cook in a 300° oven for about two hours. When it is done, weight down the top of the pâté with a brick. Chill. This wondrous pâté is a perfect first course, sliced and served with pats of sweet butter and thick slices of crusty hard rolls toasted lightly on one side only.

❧ MUSHROOM SALAD

You might prefer this after the main course. Eugene says no, you must build *up* to the squab. I have found it a perfect salad to accompany broiled chops or steak; nothing more is needed other than a hot bread.

Even canned button mushrooms are good this way. Boil as many canned or fresh whole mushrooms as are wanted along with half the amount of cubed celery in the following sauce:

to every 3 T olive or salad oil, add 1 T lemon juice, ½ t
sugar, a dash Worcestershire, salt and freshly ground pepper,
and a blade of tarragon. There should be enough sauce to
cover the mushrooms and celery. Boil briskly 5 minutes, then
chill thoroughly. Drain, but save the sauce. Shred lettuce on
individual plates, put a heaping T cottage cheese on each.
For each serving add 1 scant t pickled peach or pineapple
juice to the chilled sauce, beat well, and dribble some over
the lettuce and cheese. Pile the mushrooms and celery on the
cheese, marinate with more sauce if needed, and top with 1
t sour cream. Garnish with a few capers.

BROILED SQUAB WITH OYSTERS

Leave the squabs whole, one per person, and rub each with
lemon juice, then salt, then a generous coating of butter.
Into each cavity put an oyster that has been dipped into
butter and then into fine bread crumbs that have been lightly
browned in butter. Also put in a pitted green olive and half a
fresh, unpeeled plum. These are wonderful surprises to come
upon. Broil until done, about 30 minutes, turning them
often and basting with more butter if needed. These were
accompanied by soufflé potatoes, which I have never at-
tempted. Only a great chef—or a magician—can make them
puff up anyway.

PEARS EUGENE

Peel and core a Comice pear for each guest. Place on an individual dessert plate and, without misgiving, fill the hole of
each pear with cocoa; the cocoa will blend with the juices
so don't worry that it will taste bitter. Spread the pear completely with the following:
   This sauce must be made in advance and refrigerated at

least half a day before using. Beat one egg well, and mix with
1 cup powdered sugar, 3 T melted butter, and 1 cup of heavy
cream that has been whipped. Fold the cream in gently, and
now add a shot or two of brandy or fine rum to taste, but
remember that for *each* shot of liquor you must add an additional T of melted butter, or the sauce will be too thin. It
should be very thick and is best spread on the pear with a
spoon, to make a gala dessert not only delicious but attractive. Eugene tops each with a sprig of fresh pear leaves.

Afterward there was coffee on the long porch in small,
priceless cups which, we were told, were part of the wedding
china that had been the gift of the late Mr. Brubaker. The
moon lowered into the lake and Mrs. Brubaker murmured, "I
wonder if someone remembered to feed Nellie" (who is the
schnauzer) and with her considerable and comfortable
age for once forget herself and drowsed off in front of her
guests. We sat there murmuring among ourselves and wish-
ing everyone could be a Mrs. Brubaker and have had her
years, her ways, and a Eugene.

CHAPTER FIVE

THE LAZY DAYS

THE SUMMER CROWD is here and it is well along in June and the sailboats are out on the lake. Mrs. Brubaker has already sent out invitations for her Fourth of July dance. The farmers' fields are green; some crops have even been harvested, while you were still dreaming of spring. You pass trucks on the highway bulging with freshly picked pea vines and reach out in passing to help yourself, popping the lovely raw peas into your mouth from the pods, while the driver, expecting this ritual of early summer, grins a greeting.

A while ago the moon was full. Now a raucous catbird (trying out being everything in the world but a catbird— thrush, warbler, owl, threshing machine, pile driver) wakens you at three-thirty in the morning. You blink open reluctant eyes and find night gone. The sky is light. The catbird shrieks on, testing out timpani and cymbals now, and a presage of discomfort seems to crawl in bed beside you. The sheets are sticky. The air is heavy. The comforter under which you've slept every night is a binding weight. Suddenly from a neighbor's field comes the grinding of a tractor even more distracting than anything the catbird can manage.

The first hot days of the year have begun.

But also, the pleasant days of chilled lunches and dinners. The first really sweltering morning sends me down the road for one of Ruth Hummock's plump but not ancient hens to supply the stock for the iced soups that I can already taste like salvation against my parched tongue. The day seems no less miserable when I enter the Hummocks' crowded kitchen. Ninety-five degrees in the shade it might be, but there Ruth and John and the seven children are, scraping chairs and sitting down happily in the stifling room to a noon meal of beef roasted to a frazzle, steaming bomb-sized dumplings, oceans of thick gravy and canned peas and corn. Outside in their big truck garden, the tenderest beans sway on their vines and young peas are bursting their pods, waiting to be hauled off to market but not to be sampled by the Hummock clan; as Ruth says, stuff doesn't taste good to her bunch unless it's bought from a store. Cold foods on a blistering day? That's for picnics, Ruth says, when you can't take a stove along. And iced *soup?* At this she simply laughs kindly.

But I carry the chicken home with anticipation, knowing that because it is nicely fattened, but not yet tough, it will make the best broth. Enough stock for three or four days is always kept in the refrigerator during hot weather so that on successive days a variety of cold soups can be easily prepared —cucumber, chervil, sorrel, Summer soup or icy tomato. There is nothing more refreshing after a hot morning spent hoeing the vegetable garden without enthusiasm or accomplishment, or half-heartedly clearing a woods trail already succumbing with alarming indifference to the onslaught of dock, thistle and wild raspberry brambles. The cold soup is especially satisfying if preceded by a Daiquiri to prepare the system for the chilling pleasure to follow. Let the weeds flourish!

Let the woods trail vanish! There is more to life than slave labor under a baking sky!

ૐ ICED CUCUMBER SOUP WITH SOUR CREAM

For 1 qt. homemade chicken stock, from which the fat has
been skimmed, or 1 qt. chicken bouillon from cubes, use 2
medium unpeeled cucumbers. Dice them and simmer them
along with a small sliced onion in butter until they are tender. Add 1 cup light cream and a pinch of thyme, salt and
white pepper as needed, and simmer another 5 minutes. Rub
through a sieve into the chicken broth, add some chopped
fresh tarragon, heat again, and thicken slightly with the yolks
of 2 eggs beaten with a little of the stock. Chill thoroughly,
and garnish with a slice of lemon in each bowl and 1 t sour
cream, strewn with almonds that have been blanched, sliced
very thin, roasted brown on top of the stove in a skillet with
butter, then drained and salted. Let the almonds be still
warm. It's a pleasing contrast.

ૐ ICED CHERVIL SOUP

This is best with a stock made from a veal bone covered with
water and simmered 1 hour with a few peppercorns and
whole allspice. Add 4 or 5 peeled medium potatoes and when
they are tender rub them through a sieve and return to the
broth. Chop up a large handful of fresh chervil (or, if need
be, parsley), add to the broth and cook 15 minutes longer,
uncovered so that it remains green. Season and chill. Float
a few slices of cucumber in each cup and dust with paprika.

ૐ COLD SORREL SOUP

It's a pity this perennial is not more widely grown in our
gardens for its flavor is unique in soups, salads and stews. It

can sometimes be found in our French or Italian markets.

Into 1 qt. chicken stock put 3 potatoes, 1 carrot, salt, pepper, 2 chopped large onions and a handful of washed sorrel. When these are tender, put through a food mill or sieve. Cut another large handful of young sorrel into shreds and wilt these down in 1 T butter by covering and cooking them about 5 minutes. Add to the soup along with 1 cup light cream and serve icy cold. Garnish with thin lemon slices.

Sometimes, particularly for dinner when the soup is to be followed by cold main dishes, it is better to start with a

ह HOT SORREL SOUP

Chop together a turnip, a carrot, a leek, an onion and ½ small head of cabbage. Sprinkle with ½ t sugar and fry until pale gold in 3 T butter. Add 1 qt. chicken or veal stock and simmer 1 hour, adding more water if needed. Season well, shred very fine a sprig each of sweet basil and marjoram and a large handful of sorrel, throw them into the pot and simmer 10 minutes longer. Serve very hot with small, buttered, baking powder biscuits.

ह EUROPEAN SUMMER SOUP (OR GASPACHO)

This is a surprisingly good cold soup, and gaining popularity in this country. A strong beef broth is needed, chilled and every speck of fat skimmed off, or undiluted canned consommé may be used. No further cooking is required, and the vegetables used must be absolutely fresh. Crush a clove of garlic in a large bowl, remove it, and now add whatever fresh delights your garden offers, all very finely cubed or shredded. There must be at least ½ cup chopped raw vegetables for each cup of broth, and among these there must be peeled cucumbers, a good supply of scallions and a green pepper,

each cut very small, and ripe, ruddy tomatoes, skinned, the
seeds squeezed out, and the pulp diced. Dribble over 1½ t
real olive oil and ½ t lemon juice for each cup of broth, season with salt, fresh pepper and a dusting of sugar, and add
the broth. A sweet red pepper is also good in this; so is spinach cut into minute ribbons, small whole black olives, or any
of the salad herbs such as tarragon, chervil, parsley, basil or,
best of all, fresh dill. Serve ice-cold in ice-cold cups. One
taste on a hot day is like leaping into a cold stream. Afterward, a lazy nap.

ࣰ PREGNANT SOUP

I first tasted this noteworthy creation at the home of a pear-
shaped summer neighbor. She assured me that all pregnant
women have a passion for dill pickles. Hers was inordinate.
Hence this soup.

To 1 qt. beef stock add 1 finely minced medium onion and
either an 8 oz. can of tomato sauce or 2 cups stewed whole
tomatoes rubbed through a sieve. Cook for ½ hour to reduce
it slightly, remove from the heat but do not strain, and add
½ cup each of sweet and sour cream. Chill, and before serving add thin, short sticks of dill pickle. One medium pickle is
sufficient, if you are not pregnant. Otherwise, my friend says,
you may want more.

ࣰ HOMEMADE LIVER SAUSAGE

This wonderful and simple pâté, spread on crusty bread or
thin toast and served along with an iced soup, will make a
satisfying lunch. Cover 1½ lbs. shoulder pork with water and
boil until the meat is soft. Reserve the liquid. Boil ½ lb. pork
liver in water to cover for ½ hour, but throw this liquid
away. Grind the liver and pork together several times, add

1½ cups bread crumbs, 1 finely chopped onion, 1 T salt, ¼ t pepper, ½ t each of dried thyme and marjoram, and boil all together in the pork liquor for 10 minutes, stirring well. Cool, pack in small jars, and keep in the refrigerator. It won't remain there long, though, for you'll find it highly popular.

No sooner does the late spring season of iced soups begin, than I hunger for other cold dishes too. There is the home-made Suelze that Aunt Dell will compose on a broiling day; in some places this is called headcheese. It is spicy and aromatic, flecks of meat shaking in their jelly, and when she brings up a crock of it we feast contentedly.

Or a farm neighbor sends over a springtime offering of too many dozens of eggs for me to use up reasonably, which is the excuse for a company luncheon and a lavish egg timbale, dressed with an egg mayonnaise and sour cream and garnished with more eggs, as served and enjoyed by our farm ladies at their club meetings on their clean, shady porches. *They* can afford to use a few dozen eggs at a whack whenever they choose, with their snowy or speckled laying hens cackling all over their yards.

This is also the season of young veal for a variety of veal jellies, or cold veal with caper sauce such as Mrs. Brubaker serves at her dance buffets in her big house now that it is open for the season and summer guests are arriving. And lamb is plentiful too, and the time has come for cold, pressed lamb sandwiches for picnics under an oak tree on one of the hill-tops. With ice-cold beer at your side, you forget how the young sun has wantonly let loose its enervating rays spang in the middle of June while shrubs still bloom.

But all of these dishes are flexible. They'll serve you well either for a simple solitary lunch, or as main course following

an iced soup for a more elaborate dinner on one of those days
when even nightfall brings no stir among the shrubbery and
appetites remain laggard. Yet they are equally good as a first
course to be followed by hot dishes on more merciful evenings.

৯ EGG TIMBALES

For each six guests (and often on neighboring farms the
women invite twenty or more) boil 9 strictly fresh eggs hard,
and while still hot put the whole shelled eggs through a
ricer. Season with salt, pepper, ¼ t dry mustard, and a sprinkling either of chives or minced green onions. Pack with light
pressure into buttered timbale forms or custard cups and re-
frigerate for 3 or 4 hours. Turn out onto garden lettuce and
cover with this sauce:

Mix together ½ cup white vinegar, ½ cup water, 3 T
sugar, ½ t dry mustard, 1 t salt and 1 T flour and boil until
smooth, always stirring. Stir this gradually into 3 whole eggs,
well beaten, and cook again until it is thick, never ceasing to
stir and not letting it boil. When it has cooled, beat in ½ cup
salad oil or a little more, 1 good t paprika, 3 T chili sauce,
the juice of ½ lemon and then ½ cup thick sour cream.
Serve this tart sauce very cold over the delicate egg timbales,
and cover with the grated yolks of more hard-boiled eggs. For
a main course at dinner, serve with paper-thin slices of cold
baked ham or cold rare beef, garnished with the first peas of
the garden.

৯ HOMEMADE COUNTRY HEADCHEESE

This earthy but flavorsome dish of Aunt Dell's requires ¾
lb. veal and ¼ lb. pork, cut up fine and boiled together with

a veal bone, 1 T sugar, 1 chopped onion, salt, a few pepper-corns, a few whole allspice, and a few slices of lemon. Boil in water to cover, and when meat is almost done add white vinegar to taste. It should be quite sour. Cook until meat falls from bone, remove bone, dice the meat and return to liquor, and pour the headcheese into a stone crock to harden.

৯ VEAL ASPIC

The veal aspics are more delicate than headcheese. For a delicious clear aspic to accompany sliced cold roast veal, make a strong rich broth of veal bones, meaty but with as little fat as possible, soup greens, celery seed and ½ lemon, rind and all. Season it highly with salt, pepper, rosemary, tarragon and basil. When the broth is done, add to it the juices from roasting the veal, strain, and when cold remove all the fat. Heat again and when hot add sherry or white wine, but be cautious not to destroy the subtle flavor of the veal and herbs—the wine should only heighten it. Pour the hot broth over gelatin; 2 T dissolved in ½ cup cold broth or water for each quart of hot broth should be sufficient. Pour into a fancy wet mold and chill until hardened.

৯ JELLIED VEAL LOAF

This more sturdy aspic is a perfect first course. Cook 2 lbs. veal shank in 2 qts. water with a diced carrot, onion, piece of celery root, parsley, celery tops, salt, pepper, and a few herbs. When the meat falls from the bone, remove the bone, and cut the meat and vegetables into small pieces. Reduce the strained remaining broth to one half and pour over the meat and vegetables in a mold. Chill and serve sliced, gar-nished with deviled eggs.

ट्ट PRESSED VEAL

This, too, makes an excellent first course. The various greens
woven among the nuggets of veal will cool the spirit. Gently
boil about 4 lbs. veal knuckle and 1 onion in water to cover
until the meat is done. Trim off the meat, put it through a
food chopper and mix with it 2 T chopped parsley, 1 t
capers, 2 T chopped green or black olives and 1 T coarsely
chopped pistachio nuts. Strain the liquid in which the veal
was cooked, remove the fat, season with salt, pepper and a
dash of Madeira wine, and reduce the broth sufficiently to
jell easily—there should be just enough liquid to cover the
meat. Line a loaf pan with a few slices of hard-boiled egg,
add the meat, pour the veal broth over it and chill until firm.

ट्ट PRESSED LAMB

On a balmy June day you will enjoy a sandwich of this tender loaf, preceded by a cup of the warm broth in which the
lamb was cooked. Cover a piece of young lamb leg or shoulder with water and add seasonings of salt, pepper, sweet
marjoram, thyme and caraway seed. Boil several hours until
the meat is very tender. For the loaf, chop the lamb fine as
you would for hash, moisten with some of the broth, season
again if necessary and sprinkle with lemon juice. Put it in a
loaf pan, cover with wax paper and weight it (my neighbors
say to use an old flatiron set on a board but I use a brick—I
don't have an old flatiron) so that the meat will be firmly
packed. Chill. For the soup, to the leftover broth add a little
chopped carrot, onion, fresh parsley and rice or barley and
cook until the vegetables are done.

Any of these jellied meats will taste better still if garnished with cooked fresh or frozen vegetables, such as the

vivid broccoli or asparagus or pale cauliflower, chilled and coated either with Edna's Mayonnaise (see page 178) or a homemade oil mayonnaise. The latter is so simple to make, so excellent and bland in flavor, that one wonders why anyone would ever substitute the flavorless commercial product.

౭౿ HOMEMADE OIL MAYONNAISE

And none of the tiresome business of adding the oil drop by drop is needed here, either. I don't understand why such a fable should have been invented to discourage the making of one's own mayonnaise (or the foolish requirement that it must be beaten only with a silver fork!) for it is quick and simple to prepare. Break 1 whole egg into a bowl, and add ½ t salt, ¼ t dry mustard, and 2 or 3 T oil. I use ordinary salad oil unless the finest olive oil is available. Beat it a moment, add a few more T oil, beat again, and when it begins to thicken add the oil in large dollops until about 1 cup altogether has been added. Beat until thick, and beat in the juice of ½ lemon. I use a hand beater and it takes me less than a minute. With an electric beater it's even more of a cinch.

౭౿ COLD SLICED VEAL WITH CAPER SAUCE

With some of the above mayonnaise on hand you can prepare this easily, and I know of nothing nicer as the main dish of a cold buffet. I first tasted it at Mrs. Brubaker's Fourth of July dance where I found it on the long damask-hung table inside the panoplied tent, alongside hams and turkeys, fish mousses and chafing dishes of lobster. It was the best of all. Lard a leg of veal with butter and strips of bacon, strew over it 2 bay leaves, salt, pepper, a dozen each of peppercorns and whole allspice, and top with a few stalks of celery. Roast in a hot oven and when half done, add about 2 cups water, or water and white wine, cover it, and lower the heat to 325°. When done, cool the roast but don't chill it. Strain the juice in the pan and chill this to let it jell. Slice the roast quite thin. Over the slices pour a caper sauce:

Into the jellied veal liquor, fold a cup or so of whipped cream, depending on the amount of jelly, a generous portion of capers, ½ cup homemade mayonnaise, and 1 or 2 mashed anchovies or sardines, only enough to shade the flavor. Spread the sauce over the veal and garnish with fat black olives.

ह&• FRESH GRAPE SALAD

This also was on Mrs. Brubaker's buffet table, prepared by her chef Eugene. Make the dressing by beating 3 whole eggs along with 1 t dry mustard, 2 heaping t sugar, 1 t salt and a pinch of cayenne. Heat 1 cup light cream, but do not let it boil, add the eggs and then ½ cup hot white vinegar, stirring all the while. Cool, and when ready to serve, pour this dressing over a bowl of chopped celery, apples, and halved large seedless California grapes. Sprinkle with halved and toasted salted almonds. This is pleasing to serve with cold turkey or Aunt Dell's cold breaded pork roast (see page 182).

ह&• CURRANT GLACIER

To end a hot-weather lunch or dinner satisfyingly, mash a large package of cream cheese, stir into it 1 cup sour cream and 1 cup sweet cream whipped, sweeten to taste with confectioners' sugar (not *too* sweet) and freeze in a refrigerator tray. Fill the stem of a champagne glass with Crème de

Cassis or other fruit liqueur and over it pile the frozen cream, glacier high. Top with fresh currants or tart currant jelly.

৯ SWEET CHEESE PIE

There are two more desserts always welcome here on warm nights—rich, yet light and cooling. For a sweet cheese pie, crush 1 small box zwieback, add to it 4 T melted butter and a dash of cinnamon, and mold as a crust into an ovenproof glass pie dish. Place in refrigerator. Mix together ½ lb. cream cheese, ⅜ cup sugar, 2 eggs and ½ t vanilla. Pour into the pie shell and bake at 375° for 20 minutes. Meanwhile mix together 1 cup sour cream, 2 T sugar and ½ t vanilla. Spread this over the cooled pie and bake another 5 minutes, neither more nor less, at 475°. Chill before serving.

The second of these favored desserts is

৯ CHOCOLATE NUT PIE

When you have beaten 2 egg whites foamy, add ⅛ t each of salt and cream of tartar. Continue beating and when soft peaks form add ½ cup sugar gradually and beat until stiff. Fold in ½ cup broken walnut meats and ½ t vanilla, spread in greased pie tin and bake in a slow oven for 45 minutes. For the filling of this light, crunchy pie, melt ¼ lb. German sweet chocolate in a double boiler, and add 3 T hot water and 1 t vanilla. When this has cooled, stir in 1 cup cream, whipped. Place into the crust and chill at least 2 hours.

Then coffee, cigarettes, soft talk on the terrace. Someone yawns and says let's go dancing. Someone else would rather swim or sail. And after a cooling dinner such as one of the above, on a hot June day that lingers on into the twilight, you glance out toward the plum trees and see that instead of bright blooms (when did they go—a week ago? two weeks? and why didn't you mark their passing?) there are nodules of pale green fruit covering the branches. You hadn't noticed: summer itself has already begun.

PART TWO

THE
RIPENING
SUMMER

CHAPTER ONE

THE COUNTRY HOTEL

NEARBY STANDS THE country hotel, open now for the summer season. Actually it has been open all year round, harboring a few hunters or skiers through the blizzards of winter, and transient salesmen during the softening rains of spring. But it is in the summertime that the old place flourishes. Windows are flung open to air the rooms, the porch gets a coat of paint. Happiest of all, since Decoration Day the sign has been hanging again from the front pillar: EAT HERE— MEALS FAMILY STYLE—WELCOME.

Our hotel is called the Majestic and has stood in its grove of shade trees since the turn of the century, perhaps majestic then but not in such majesty now. Its garden is neglected, though tiger lilies poke through the tall grass on summer days, and the unkempt bushes loyally shade the porches from the July sun. Yet it is still a lovely hotel, of cream brick, square, with many long porches, its windows tall.

It is no longer stylish, though a few old stand-bys from Chicago or Milwaukee return each summer, seeming to sit all day in the shade, remembering, the women knitting, and after the heavy noon meal napping upstairs in the big, airy bed-

rooms. But mostly now it harbors only a few traveling vaca-
tioners. Andy, the proprietor, fat, lazy and welcoming, rocks
the hot months away on the porch and in some seasons with
unexpected energy, perhaps as a tribute to past glory, plants
up the circular front flower bed with bright red cannas bor-
dered by bright nasturtiums.

But sometimes on a summer Sunday the creaky hotel will
be taken over in toto, grounds and all, for a reunion of one of
the neighboring farm families. Then it is clamorously alive
again. There are ball games in the grove behind the hotel
for the young people, contests, loud talk. Cars continue to arrive, as they have all morning, some from long distances, for
the great family conclave; there are shouts of recognition,
news is exchanged, faces remembered. Some of the older,
shirt-sleeved men start pinochle or sheepshead games in the
bar (more properly, the saloon, for it is of the vintage of
smoothly carved, mahogany-breasted women and long etched
mirrors). On the porch outside, the wives visit in busy remi-
niscence and fan themselves with their handkerchiefs.

But through corridors and barroom and porches and grove
there is an air of waiting. Andy's hotel is popular for these
gatherings with reason. From the dining room for the past
hour has come the clink of glasses and cutlery. The open windows of the big back kitchen exhale fragrances—simmering
pork tenderloins or the chicken stew with celery root and
baked stuffing for which Andy's wife is famous. And everyone
in the county knows that Andy's brother-in-law owns the
local slaughterhouse, which means that the choicest meats
are available to him.

By a few minutes before twelve o'clock the waiting is un-
comfortable. The ball game has been abandoned in indifference. Men idle out of the bar. Children are cranky. The

women have forgotten their subjects of conversation and merely smile back and forth at each other. Everyone knows something wondrous is about to happen when, promptly at noon, Andy takes out his pocket watch.

"I suppose you folks need some nourishment," he says lazily (as though he didn't know) and opens the double plate-glass doors with their thick net curtains.

Most appealing of all the Majestic's many chambers is its dining room. Its glory is well earned. Every Sunday, during summer, it relives its openhearted past. Our countryside, because of the influx of Lake residents from Decoration Day to Labor Day, is well supplied with attractive (and expensive) eating places. But none has such gusto or offers the pleasures of the Majestic. The fancier places, with their tasteful window boxes and white-coated bus boys and circular bars, seem to thrive on monotony: one would think the American diet consisted solely of steaks, fried chicken, or rock lobster tails, for their menus rarely offer anything else. And along with these dishes? Your choice: French fried or American; frozen peas or string beans; Roquefort or Thousand Island dressing.

Not so in the long, cool, shady, dining hall of the old country hotel. First of all, whether it be a clan gathering of fifty invading the dining room, or a transient family of four motoring by on a sunny Sunday (or myself, happily hurrying down on the stroke of noon with a friend or two), you don't order. You eat, and with delight, what is served you, family style. Neither Andy nor his wife has betrayed any guest yet.

The plates and glasses are thick but the cloths are snowy white. The chairs are high-backed and venerable. The walls are wainscoted and darkish still-lifes hang in imitation walnut frames. And, on the tables, there are platters of the famed chicken and celery root stew (the platters replenished before

72   THE RIPENING SUMMER

the need arises) or the equally delicious pork tenderloins simmered in stock and cream, mountains of fresh corn on the
cob, kidney bean and lentil salad, hot homemade rolls, sliced
and unadorned ruby-red tomatoes, preserves, pickles; fresh
raspberry or peach or blueberry shortcake for dessert.

The assembled clan eats with enthusiasm, as do I and any
guests I have ever taken there, and the platters empty miracu-
lously. After dinner the old hotel grows somnolent, the clatter
gradually dies in the kitchen and Andy's wife's seven cats doze
on the back stoop. The bulging young men try to resume their
ball game but pretend it's too hot and soon snooze under the
elm trees. In the barroom, the men play cards again but with
little more interest than that of the women trying to pick up
the dropped stitches of their conversation on the porch.

Everyone is sated. You'd think they'd go home. But actually what all are waiting for is suppertime, when the orgy is
repeated: long platters of cold meats or an inspired hamburger casserole (unfortunately called Yum-yum), bowls of
potato salad with cucumber and hard-boiled egg, sauce dishes
of stewed fruits, piles of bread. It grows all too clear that anyone who frequents the dining hall of the Majestic must not
take his meals lightly.

I have found Andy's wife's recipes useful on more than
one occasion. Once one moves to the country, friends and
relatives never waver in their belief that you've built the house
only for their pleasure on balmy summer week ends. New lug-
gage is acquired overnight, new automobiles, road maps with
routes leading directly to your door, and a new love of country living. *You* have become proprietor of a country hotel.

Sometimes you wonder how the dinner table will hold

them all. There are those visitors who never make their beds, lose their trout flies in your soup pot and sprinkle cigarette ashes on your clean hearth. But there are also those proper and welcome visitors who will make you swell with pride because you own these hills, those trees, this house. With city-starved eyes they see the beauty of the meadow grasses, growing silvery tan with summer. The wail of a screech owl on a dark August night is a thrilling sound they have gladly traveled many miles to hear. Your garden peas are the sweetest ever grown. And Ruth Hummock's hens (for by mid-August she will begin to kill them) are the juiciest, plumpest ever raised.

For such guests you do not mind the labor of preparing meals for a dozen extra. (These friends even help with dishes.) I have grown able to sniff the Saturday morning air and tell whether several carloads of hungry, unexpected, week end visitors are going to turn into the drive. The recipes from the old hotel have proved invaluable for these large groups or for large picnics (planned or impromptu); when the crowd grows cumbersome, we cook in electric roasters and carry the steaming dinner out to the hills. These dishes are not too difficult to prepare in quantity and they can be cooked in advance and reheated when needed.

ࣔ CHICKEN AND CELERY ROOT STEW

Into a stew pot or electric roaster put as many pieces of young plump hens as required, figuring ¾ lb. per person unless your friends eat like pigs, which is apt to happen in the country. (Andy's wife also puts in a few feet for extra flavor and color.) Just cover with water and keep it at this level and no more, remembering that you are making stew, not soup. Add a few bay leaves, whole allspice and peppercorns, salt, and 1 small sliced onion, 1 carrot, and 1 t paprika for each hen. A dash of lemon juice is good too. Peel celery roots, cut into small dice, about 1 cup per hen, and add to the stew ½ hour before the hen is tender, along with some of the finely shredded celery root leaves (these are strong and fresh-flavored). Before serving, reduce the gravy if necessary, thicken with cornstarch, remove the skins from the meat if you like, and add a good handful of chopped parsley to make the stew as green and lush as summertime itself.

You may think it a surfeit of celery, but excellent with this stew are hearts of celery stuffed with a paste made of the fowl livers, fried in butter and mashed with a little mayonnaise, lemon juice and fresh chives. And indispensable with the stew is

৯ BAKED CORNBREAD STUFFING

This will take the place of both potatoes and bread. It can be mixed beforehand and baked while the chicken is stewing. A day or two before, bake as much cornbread as is needed, using the package mix if you like. When needed, crumble into a large bowl, and to each average size cornbread add 3 or 4 pieces stale white bread and 3 or 4 hard rolls or stale biscuits. Soak this in broth from the stewing hens or stock made from the giblets. Season well with salt, pepper and a pinch of poultry seasoning, 1 chopped onion and a little parsley. Add 1 cup creamed corn and a few T cooked rice. Mash the mixture well and beat in 2 eggs. Bake in a hot pan or skillet greased with bacon fat, having sprinkled 2 T diced bacon over the stuffing. Keep moist if necessary with fat and broth skimmed from the stew and bake until a golden crust forms.

ح PORK TENDERLOIN IN BROTH AND CREAM

For each six persons brown 2 lb. tenderloin in chicken fat or half butter and half bacon fat. Separately brown ½ lb. sliced mushrooms. Put both into a roaster along with 1 clove minced garlic, 1 can consommé diluted with ½ can water, 2 fresh peeled tomatoes (or 2 canned, well strained), salt, pepper and some pieces of parsley. Cover and bake slowly for 2 hours. During the last 10 minutes, add ½ cup cream. Thicken the gravy with flour that has been lightly browned in a skillet, and serve the meat right in the sauce. Sometimes I boil tiny new potatoes separately, skin them, and add them to the roaster at the last minute. Then, along with a bagful of radishes and scallions, our whole dinner is ready to be transported anywhere in the woods we choose. We haul chilled red wine along.

ح YUM-YUM

Despite its obnoxious name this dish has never failed to please all comers. It is inexpensive, easy to prepare by the roasterful on crowded Sundays, and needs no more than a salad to complete it. For each pound of hamburger (serving 4 guests) plan to use 1 cup coarsely chopped onion, 1 cup chopped celery, ½ chopped green pepper, 1 can mushroom soup diluted with ½ can water, and a 3 oz. can chow mein noodles. Brown the meat to a good crisp brown in butter, while the onions, celery and pepper are frying in more butter or oil until pale gold. Season lightly, mix together in a casserole, rinse out both pans with a little water to get out all the juices, pour over and add the soup and remaining water. Cover and bake in a moderate oven 45 minutes. Remove cover, spread the noodles on top and allow to heat through.

ફ્જ KIDNEY BEAN AND LENTIL SALAD
On hot summer Sundays we serve this with a cold roast and
piles of fresh bread-and-butter sandwiches. With 1 can well-
drained but not rinsed kidney beans, mix 1 cup cooked lentils, ½ green pepper and 1 medium onion (chopped fine),
½ cup chopped celery heart and ¼ cup pecan halves. Chill
to an icy crispness and ½ hour before ready to serve moisten
liberally with homemade mayonnaise (see page 63) into
which you have stirred the juice of ½ lemon, ½ t each of
sugar and prepared mustard, and a dash of Worcestershire.
Crumble crisp bacon over the top.

One Sunday dawned blessedly rainy. There was no likeli-
hood of visitors that day. We could rest and dawdle. But by
early afternoon the sky suddenly revealed sun and bouncing
clouds. An hour later a car raced up the hill. Soon another
. . . "It turned out to be such a heavenly day we thought
we'd just run out from town."

This day, however, we had no provisions. A picnic would
be the simplest solution but we had little to picnic with. A
call to Andy for help only made the day seem more dismal
while the sky grew more and more radiant. Andy had a reunion on his hands and because of the rain everyone had simply stayed on in the dining room that noon, eating until every
pot in the kitchen was empty. But possibly his wife could fix
up some sandwiches. . . .

A big basketful arrived. I don't like sandwiches. But
along with a carton of potato salad Andy's wife filched out of
the supper ration, these came as pheasant and champagne.
They have since become staple (and hungered-for) picnic fare
and are the only picnic sandwiches I've ever found edible. No
cold cuts slapped between weary slices of bread are these.

❧ CHOPPED HAM AND LEAF LETTUCE SANDWICHES ON RYE BREAD

Cream ⅓ cup butter until very soft, add the yolk of 1 egg, 1 good T prepared mustard, pepper, salt, and mix well. Then stir in as much ground, boiled ham as is needed (about ¾ lb.) to give it a smooth spreading consistency. Take this from the refrigerator an hour before using, or the butter will harden it. Spread a slice of finest rye bread with this, spread another with butter, and place fresh leaf lettuce in between. And Andy's wife warns you not to settle for any other lettuce, particularly iceberg. It doesn't feel right.

I've discovered that corned beef or pastrami are also excellent to use in these sandwiches, instead of ham.

❧ VEAL WALDORF SANDWICHES

Make a regular Waldorf salad (though dicing it well) of apples, celery, walnut pieces and mayonnaise. Season it well, especially with freshly ground pepper. Add to this ⅓ the amount of cold roast veal, finely cubed, and spread between buttered pieces of white bread. Be sure the bread has a good crust.

❧ VEAL AND SLAW SANDWICHES

Either a light rye bread or white is good for these. Butter a piece of bread, place on it a layer of thinly sliced cold roast veal, season well and spread generously with homemade mayonnaise. On this, place a layer of coleslaw (see page 174) and top with a second piece of lightly buttered bread. You'll have a husky yet wonderfully delicate sandwich.

One more dish is indispensable to those who find their country homes acquiring the popularity of a summer hotel.

And it is the dish most fun to make, for it is cooked outdoors and requires that all hands, young and old, be put to work daylong to assist in its preparation. A week-end guest first suggested we experiment with it and it has since become an annual midsummer rite. She had the recipe from her aunt in Mississippi, beginning, "Take two hens, twelve doves, a squirrel and several partridges. . . ."

However—

₹➤ MEADOW STEW (FOR TWENTY-FIVE PEOPLE)

Forswear the doves and partridges. Dig a large pit in a lovely meadow and start a good fire in it before dawn. An event such as making meadow stew should be celebrated with much commotion; if you have only a dozen guests, call in the neighbors. Children are necessary. Also dogs. In the shade near the fire pit, set up long work tables; here, while the men reduce the fire to incandescent coals, set the women and children to the task of shelling garden peas and limas and (if in season) scraping milky kernels of corn from their cobs. Let them chop cabbages. Put 2 gallons of water into a large pot or scoured wash boiler and when it is bubbling add 2 lbs. each of veal shank, pork shank, beef shank and breast of lamb. Now throw in a fat hen. And if a guest has been able to produce a squirrel or rabbit from the woods, either makes a wonderful addition; we sometimes add the frozen domestic rabbit.

Simmer all this slowly until the meat is tender. It is then taken from the broth, cooled, boned and chopped by the women, then returned to the pot. With it go 3 large potatoes, 6 carrots, a dozen onions, 2 green peppers, a peck of tomatoes and a head of cabbage, all chopped. Then 2 hot red pepper pods, several handfuls of lima beans or a pack of the frozen, a few cups of fresh or canned corn, and a good bunch of parsley. Salt it well and add more water or tomato juice if needed. Add 4 t Worcestershire sauce. Everyone now must take turns stirring the stew for another hour or so until it is thick. As the day wanes, serve in large bowls to your starving friends with a shaker of chili powder on the table. There really should be fireworks later.

CHAPTER TWO

FRIENDS THAT PASS
IN THE NIGHT

BEST OF ALL I love summer nights. Summer unrolls its green-
ery only for the too beneficent sun to scorch. Were man wiser
he would sleep from ten in the morning to four in the afternoon during these months of doldrum. These are the hours
of glare, road dust, parched insect noises and failing appetite.

The trees look stunned. But with late afternoon dew returns the sheen to grass and shrubs. The moonvines open,
writhing to unfold their glistening and fragrant saucers of
flower right before your eyes. By darktime—with the children
alive again too, hollering over their games in the distant village—the earth is recapturing its equilibrium. I think cows
moo in summer twilights only with pleasure because night is
coming. In the dark you can hear trees stirring, breathing
their relief. With each moment a new sound of reviving life is
added. Appetites return. The world is freshest at midnight—
this is the happiest hour for night-people like myself.

A car turns through the gateway and starts up the hill,
and then another. You flash on the yard lights. Tanned girls
step from the cars; the men wear neckties and shoes (hard

80

concessions to make in the country in the summertime). But
these are all night-people too: some are members of the summer stock company playing nearby, hungry now after a per-
formance; others are city friends who have driven out to see
the show invited to stop by here for a few long drinks and
some supper on their way back to town. There is a special
gaiety in starting a party at this dark, calm hour when much
of the world is already asleep. Farmers around us will be wak-
ing when the last guest yawns and leaves.

Actors are always hungry at midnight. Their talk over
their first highballs or beers is relaxing and exciting. There is a
peculiar pleasure for the host as well in entertaining at this
hour. It has meant puttering around the kitchen all evening,
getting things ready. But since buffet dishes—and buffet it
will be—can be prepared entirely beforehand, now that the
party is ready to start, so is he.

Somebody plays the piano. Somehow in every stock company, large or small, celebrated or unheralded, there is one
member who can play with as engaging sophistication as any
pianist murmuring in a New York cocktail lounge. The city
people at first look remote. But soon they have magically been
blown into the core of the party. My city friends try blush-
ingly to act like theater people and the actors try to act simple
and human and you don't know which is the nicer group. By
the third drink you don't know which is which. More than
likely the character woman has taken off her shoes, the juvenile is squatting on the floor with a banker's wife, and the
ingénue is using all her Bankhead wiles on the banker (and doing all right). Words and phrases cross and recross:

voices: *Streetcar* . . . Cornell and McClintic . . . strike the
   set . . .

LEADING LADY: My God, did you see how I loused up my second-act entrance?

VOICES: Next season . . . next season . . . I think I'll try TV this winter, what do you think, too commercial? . . . I'll trade Gerry Page for Hepburn any day but which Hepburn do you mean, Katie or Audrey? . . .

HEAVY: I can't stand this smell of food any longer! When do we eat?

It's an easy, lovely, and oddly distinguished party. For it, you try to provide a supper to match. There are certain combinations of foods that always prove most popular at these parties. On a hot night, out on the quiet, kerosene-torchlit terrace, it's likely to be cold eggs in a spicy sauce, a warm pot of Swedish beans, a chilled meat loaf inlaid with a mosaic of cheese, and the inevitable hit—a great platter of Russian meat salad that should always be relished with icy beer.

On a cool night there will be one or two hot casserole dishes. From these, guests help themselves, then gather around the long oak table stretched to its full length in the kitchen. Potatoes and carrots creamed together, much more savory than it sounds, bound together with a mushroom sauce; or a more spectacular water chestnut casserole, either of these served with nothing more than cold roast or fowl.

Should it be an intermediate night of warmth, when the charcoal grill is being used on the arbored back terrace, the proper dish always seems to be a thick, grilled, sugared ham steak, while on a table nearby in the shadows the chafing dish is waiting with a beer rarebit (into which too many guests already, you notice, have stuck probing fingers).

And the talk is even faster, higher-pitched now, until you'd think you were right back in New York City instead of on a hilltop surrounded by sleeping farmers and their wives and broods.

BANKER: Can you really learn *all* those lines every week all by yourself, Miss Y? . . .

VOICES: Royalties . . . Equity . . . Laurette Taylor—there was a woman. . . .

CHARACTER WOMAN: Has anyone seen my shoe?

JUVENILE: Might the Lunts really come to see the play next week? How terrifying!

VOICES: ANTA . . . City Center . . . Fonda . . .

INGÉNUE: Oh, I only had this little part last season on Broadway but Brooks Atkinson said . . .

VOICES: Anyone—seen—shoe? . . . *When* do we eat? . . .

(*Exeunt to terrace or kitchen*) for

BUFFET FOR A HOT NIGHT

ঽ EGGS AND MUSTARD SAUCE

Boil hard as many eggs as are wanted. Let them cool, shell them, cut in half lengthwise, arrange on a platter with parsley garnish. Make a sauce by melting 2 T butter and blending into it 2 T flour, 2 T sugar, a pinch of salt and 2 t ground mustard. Slowly stir in 1 cup water and 2 T vinegar and cook until thick. This spicy-sweet sauce should be poured warm over the cool eggs when ready to serve. It should be enough for about a dozen egg halves. Fresh tarragon leaves are good strewn over the eggs.

ঽ SWEDISH BROWN BEANS

If the imported Swedish beans are not available, use dried kidney beans. Put on 1 lb. to boil in cold water and simmer until they are tender or about 3 hours, adding more water if necessary. Add to them a minced onion, ¼ cup dark brown sugar, ¼ cup red wine, a small chunk of butter, 2 T lemon juice and salt to taste. Simmer 10 minutes longer. If need be, thicken with 1 T flour mixed with a little of the liquid. Garnish with raw onion rings.

ଈ VEAL AND CHEESE LOAF

This is a festive-looking loaf. Mix 2 lbs. ground veal with 1½ cups cubed sharp American cheese, 1 large onion and 1 large green pepper, chopped, 1 cup bread crumbs, 2 t salt, 1 t fresh pepper, another of celery salt and a pinch of cayenne, and moisten the whole with 2 eggs beaten with 3 cups milk. Pack into a greased loaf pan and bake about 1½ hours in a moderate oven. Chill, turn on to a platter and coat the loaf with cream cheese softened at room temperature. Decorate with sliced stuffed olives.

ଈ RUSSIAN SALAD

This magnificent, hearty salad is really sufficient unto itself if served with buttered black bread, cucumber sticks, and a side platter of herring dressed with sour cream and onion rings. If served as part of a large buffet, your supper will become imperial.

Leftover meat may be used—leg of lamb or veal, roast beef, baked ham or rare sirloin steak. Use at least two kinds, slice it no thicker than ⅛″, and cut these into narrow ribbons. Make more than you think you'll need because if there is any left, which is unlikely, it will keep well in the refrigerator. Now to the meat add an equal amount of assorted sausage cut in thin julienne; be sure there is a variety of texture in the sausages—some soft such as thick Bologna or

Mortadella, some hard and chewy such as summer sausage. Next comes dill pickle, these too cut into matchstick size. Use them cautiously and yet generously. But that's not all: now add tiny pickled pearl onions and some capers, just enough of each so their presence is unmistakable. Mix it all together with only the finest homemade mayonnaise (see page 63) and serve it chilled, mounded on your most spectacular platter.

BUFFET FOR A COOL NIGHT

ह्ठ CREAMED POTATOES AND CARROTS

This will pleasantly accompany a baked ham or cold sliced sirloin of beef or beef tenderloin. Melt 2 T butter, blend in 2 T flour, add 1½ cups milk and dissolve in this 1 bouillon cube and a package of dehydrated mushroom soup. Season well. This should not be a pallid dish, and sometimes I add a pinch of curry or cayenne, or fresh marjoram or chives or grated cheese. Pour into a casserole in which you have mixed 3 cups diced potatoes, 1 cup thinly sliced carrots and a small minced onion. Add more milk if necessary to cover the vegetables, place 4 strips bacon over the top and bake 1 hour in a moderate oven.

ह्ठ WATER CHESTNUT CASSEROLE

Cut a bunch of Pascal celery into 1″ pieces. Cook in a large 14 oz. can of chicken broth (or in homemade broth if you have it, of course) until it is nearly tender. Be careful not to let it get soft. Thicken the broth with 2 T cornstarch, season, pour it and the celery into a casserole and add 1 can water chestnuts, sliced, and ¼ cup blanched, slivered almonds.

Sprinkle with bread crumbs, dot with butter, and bake ½ hour in a moderate oven. You'll find this unusual dish, with its crunchy surprises, perfect to serve with cold fowl or a cold roast.

A GRILLED MIDNIGHT SUPPER

ॐ GRILLED SUGARED HAM STEAK

Use the finest center cut ham steak you can find. It should be 1" thick, which will be enough to serve five or six. Place on the grill over a slow, steady bed of charcoal. Dust the topside lightly with powdered cloves, then spread it rather generously with prepared mustard and sprinkle it with a small handful of brown sugar. Grill for 5 minutes, turn, and again treat the top with cloves, mustard and sugar. Repeat this every 5 minutes until the ham is done; it should have a dark, fragrantly sweet crust and be a juicy, delicate pink inside. When serving, slice crosswise *very* thin.

Let one of your guests, under your supervision, grill the ham steak for you while you, on a small table nearby, are performing over a chafing dish the impressive rites of making a really good

ॐ BEER RAREBIT

Nothing will do for this but a truly aged, sharp, American Cheddar cheese. A good rarebit simply can't be made with processed cheese. It is a dismaying truth that cheese companies would not produce these pallid, rubbery substances if consumers did not buy them in staggering quantities. Yet every city has a cheese store where honest-to-goodness, mellow cheeses await the buyer willing to look for them. So find an honorable, bitey, golden wheel of Cheddar, and for each pound of this cheese melt 2 T butter in a chafing dish, blend in 1 T flour and then 1 cup beer. Add a dash of ground mustard. Into this slowly melt the cheese, either cubed or grated, stirring all the while. Fleck the sauce with freshly ground pepper and paprika, add a few capers and serve on firm, dry toast. With this, the ham steak, and a platter of sliced fresh tomatoes doused with lemon juice, salt, pepper and shredded fresh basil or tarragon leaves, you will have a midnight supper on which even the intemperate, maddening moon will smile down.

Sometimes the hour is reversed. I often ask friends for supper before the theater (all of us to go on to the play later); and any of the above menus is as good then, easy to prepare and simple to serve after a few cocktails—or even along with cocktails, since curtain time always comes too soon and you must dash for the playhouse while you've still barely lifted the third olive out of your Martini glass.

At times, though, there is need for a more solid supper. City friends have put in a hard day's work. Cold eggs or a cold drumstick won't suffice. There are three menus good to serve then, but even these can in most part be prepared beforehand. They are popular for Sunday suppers even without the theater afterward, casually served, casually eaten and, always important especially in summertime, little strain on the host. The first is:

&ぅ VEAU À LA CRÈME

Cut several pounds of sliced veal steak into serving pieces, season, and brown in butter, but do not let it get darker than pale gold. Sprinkle liberally with paprika and remove from

fire. In another skillet cook very slowly a great mass of sliced
onions (at least 4 or 5) but these also must not get brown.
They should be cooked a long time, stirring them often, until they are reduced to a moist, transparent pulp. Put this
over the veal steak, pour over 1 cup sweet cream, cover, and
cook on a low flame on top the stove for at least an hour.
Add more cream if necessary. The steak should be tender
enough to cut with a fork, and the cream and onions trans-
formed to a velvety, subtle sauce. Serve this with rice or
noodles and

৪৯ COLD BROCCOLI WITH ARNOSTI
ITALIAN DRESSING
The friend who taught me this, Mrs. Arnosti, says that only
fresh broccoli can be used, never frozen. Cook one bunch of
broccoli until just tender in as little water as possible. Drain
absolutely dry and chill, saving the liquor in which the broccoli steamed. Reduce this to ½ cup and chill. Boil 2 eggs
for 3 minutes only, crumble very fine with a fork, add salt
and 3 T olive oil and blend thoroughly, whipping with a
fork. Add pepper, 1 t sugar, 1 t chives or parsley, 2 T wine
vinegar and the broccoli liquor. Serve over the broccoli, garnished with sliced radishes.

Any simple dessert, such as lemon sherbet with a touch of
white crème de menthe, will complete these menus. The second, also using veal, is:

৪৯ VEAL AND MUSHROOMS IN SOUR CREAM
Nicely brown 2½ lbs. veal steak, pounded thin and cut into
2″ pieces, in butter. Season well with salt, pepper, 1 T paprika, a sprinkling of lemon juice, add 1 cup water and if you

like a small chunk of anise, cover, and simmer about 40 minutes or until tender. Be sure there is always enough liquid in the pan to make a good gravy. Add ½ lb. fresh mushrooms, halved and lightly fried in butter, and cook 10 minutes longer. Stir in 1 cup sour cream and heat only. Sometimes I add a few cooked garden peas, but this is only for color. It is convenient to keep this warm and serve from a chafing dish; and it should always be served with fried green cabbage (see page 97) and a spoon bread, though this requires some last minute fussing in the kitchen. But it is worth it: the three flavors intertwine like graces.

❧ SPOON BREAD

This cannot be mixed in advance and it must be served the moment it is ready or it will fall flat. Either white or yellow corn meal may be used, but white and preferably waterground is always better. There are two methods for preparing a spoon bread.

The simpler (if life among your friends on the terrace is too enchanting to tear yourself away for long) is: scald 2 cups of milk; when it begins to boil, add 2 T butter, ½ t salt, and stir in ½ cup corn meal—it won't lump if you trickle it in slowly. When this has thickened break in 2 whole unbeaten eggs and mix well. Pour into a greased glass casserole about 7″ across and bake until risen and browned, about ½ hour, in a 375° oven.

The second, and more delicious, method is to mix 1 cup corn meal with 1 cup cold milk. Scald 2 cups milk, add 1 t salt, 3 T butter, and slowly stir into it the corn meal and cold milk mixture. Keep stirring and when it has thickened remove from fire. Add 3 egg yolks, beat well with a spoon, and add 1 t baking powder. Then fold in 3 egg whites, beaten very stiff. Bake in a large greased casserole in a 375° oven about 50 minutes or until it is puffed and golden. Serve now, without having just one more quick cocktail.

And the third of these menus is:

৪৯ PORK TENDERLOIN WITH CURRANT SAUCE
Salt and pepper 2 lbs. of pork tenderloins, leaving them whole (this should serve five or six) and brown them in butter. Place in a casserole, sprinkle with rosemary, spread over them ½ cup butter and add a large glass of currant jelly. Bake covered for 40 minutes in a moderate oven. Add 1 cup cream in which you have blended 1 T flour and cook 10 minutes longer. Serve this under the stars with rice, a Bibb lettuce salad and a full-bodied red wine—while fireflies glimmer down the meadow, you'll learn to love the summer night as I do.

CHAPTER THREE

SUMMER FULLNESS

KOHLRABI AND CARROTS and summer squash. Tomatoes and string beans. Kale. Lettuces: Boston, Bibb and leaf. Satiny eggplant the color of plums and tall, green broccoli. Suddenly in midsummer the garden is rife with produce. It is now that the country dweller knows glory: the vegetable plot has reached its peak, spilling plenty from every bush and vine.

You eat first with impatient curiosity, then ecstasy, then repletion, until you swear not to open another seed catalogue next winter—for you yourself, with hoe and ardor, have wrought all this plenitude. Your nights grow nightmarish with puzzling over how to consume, can, freeze or otherwise dispose of basketfuls of beets and beans. Yet by early morning, the air smiling and dewy, you are up harvesting again, only to have a young tender cabbage plump to maturity right behind your back—a moment before you'd thought it was only a Brussels sprout. Then you load up your car. You'll deposit all these wonders at the doorstep of one of your neighbors. On the highway you pass your neighbor, delivering tubfuls of produce to *you*.

Nevertheless, a truly fresh vegetable, decently prepared,

is something to experience: corn rushed from the field to the
boiling pot and husked on its way, tomatoes warm from the
sun and ready to drop from the bush in fat ripeness, yellow
and green beans so crisp they snap in your fingers as you
gather them. Vegetables become new personalities in the
country. City visitors often speak unkindly of carrots. (Much
maligned by them too, and neglected, are cabbages and kohl-
rabies, which can be lovely, tender things.) But too often the
city markets supply only carrots the size of baseball bats and
as durable; then, city cooks and restaurateurs boil them in
torrents of water and smother them in lumpy cream sauce; or
they mismate them with peas and serve both victims
drowned in a soupy liquid like bodies washed ashore.

A young carrot, pulled when it is still slim and only three
or four inches long, slivered and gently cooked with a few
sprigs of fresh mint, is something else again. We served them
this way one summer, the fresh mint flavor pervasive but yet
not quite definable, to a doubting New York guest firm in her
belief that all carrots were fodder. A month later, back East, a
disturbing conviction grew in her that life would have little direction unless she could taste carrots with mint again. She
found the young carrots, all right, without too much diffi-
culty. But though she journeyed from shop to shop she could
find no fresh mint. She even looked hungrily, and slyly, into
neighbors' window boxes. No luck.

But she was not without resources. In final desperation
our friend went to the Plaza bar, ordered a mint julep; she
tucked the fresh mint used for a garnish into her purse when
no one was looking, and with a sense of triumph downed the
julep, purring like a contented carrot. In fact, the mint looked
skimpy so she had two juleps, and went home feeling fine.

The carrots-and-mint for her dinner that night were fine too, she thinks.

ಶಿ CARROTS AND FRESH MINT

Slice young lean carrots into thin 2″ sticks, or if they are very small keep them whole, and cook them in no more than 2 or 3 T pure butter and an equal amount of water. Cover and cook gently; sometimes it takes no longer than 5 or 6 minutes for them to become tender. Then the cover is lifted to let the remaining water, if any, steam away. Salt, freshly ground pepper, and half a dozen or more of fresh, shredded mint leaves are added along with a few crumbs of brown sugar. Sauté a moment longer, shaking the pan. The mint flavor should be elusive, so don't add too many leaves—just enough to make guests wonder what the seasoning is.

Happily today, as this friend learned, excellent fresh vegetables can be found in cities. All towns have summer farmers' markets and the country abounds with roadside stands; even a pocket-sized city now has one of the remarkable supermarkets where, with careful shopping, vegetables can be found not too long ago removed from the earth in which they were grown. The great cities, of course, have shop after shop where the finest produce can be found though sometimes the best of these shops, managed by loving and thoughtful Italians or Frenchmen or Greeks, are tucked in far-off corners. It's fun to hunt them out.

But even so, good vegetables are too often negligently cooked and might just as well have come from a can in the first place, for all you can tell by the flavor. Modern cookery seems to have become a tired ritual: cook in one cup water, drain (usually not too carefully, and nothing is worse), add butter and salt. A deadening sameness lurks over the vegetable platter and bowls, even in otherwise discerning households and restaurants. Certainly no honest bean nor spear of broccoli nor any of the vegetables, should ever be "doctored up"; rather, their true, and too often hidden or destroyed, flavor should be brought out to its fullest.

The methods of cooking garden vegetables are infinite. For some of them, even frozen products will cast no shadow of shame on the first-rate cook—it is the *regard* with which the vegetable is prepared that counts. At all times, unless the liquor is wanted for sauces, only the smallest amount of water should be used: sometimes only a tablespoon or two, no more than is necessary to get by without scorching, and if possible even that steamed away at the end, rather than draining off any of the delectable natural flavors.

Once, for several months, I had a cook who held no faith in cooking without floods of water. Her dream of heaven must have been a place lined with faucets. If a two-quart pot did not hold enough water for Mrs. Becksmith to boil to disintegration a small cup of peas or the tenderest morsels of new potato, she resolutely went off into the routine of parboiling "to get out the bitter taste." Spinach, chard, green beans, zucchini, all alike found themselves accused of harboring bitter venoms inside them. The gentle vegetables found themselves churning and tossing like wrecked ships in a pot filled to the brim. Then the water was tossed like a freshet down the sink, the pot refilled. Back on the roaring flame until the water again foamed and spouted. Three times this was repeated until Mrs. Becksmith settled down to a calmer procedure of boiling all hell out of whatever was left in the pot for another half hour. She was also the grouchiest woman I have ever known, but hers is a story to continue in a later chapter.

੬๖ GREEN BEANS IN CREAM AND CHICKEN BROTH

Cook 1 lb. fresh French-cut green beans until barely tender, and reduce the liquor in which they cooked to only a few tablespoons. Place the beans in a shallow casserole and sprinkle with salt and pepper. Cover with a layer of onion rings shaved as thinly as possible. Make a light sauce of 2 T butter, 1½ T flour, and ¾ cup chicken broth or bouillon. Add ⅓ cup cream and the bean liquor. Pour over the beans, sprinkle very lightly with grated Swiss cheese (no more than 1 T) and a few dabs of butter, and bake in a hot oven until bubbly.

੬๖ OLD-FASHIONED GREEN BEANS

This delicious method of Aunt Dell's requires not only the freshest beans of the garden (frozen won't do), but sauce dishes from which to eat them. Dice and brown lightly ¼ lb. bacon, and to it add 1 lb. fresh green or snap beans, salt, pepper, and about 1 cup water. Cook for a few minutes before adding a small handful of green onions and 2 young medium-sized potatoes, pared and diced. Cook covered for another half hour until all is very tender. The liquor counts in this so don't feel traitorous in boiling the vegetables longer than is usually necessary. Ladle the vegetables and their juices into big sauce dishes and eat with a spoon. Here in the country we find this a highly satisfactory lunch along with any of the corn breads or fried corn cakes (see page 44).

༄ STRING BEANS IN DRIPPINGS

You'll find these a wonderful surprise to accompany roast beef. Put ¼ cup beef drippings into a skillet, add about 1 lb. green beans, salt, pepper and a little thyme, and cook covered over a low flame. Add no water unless it is needed to keep them from burning and steam them in this manner until they are perfectly tender. When done, sprinkle lightly with flour and stir in enough soup broth to moisten them well.

༄ SWEET-SOUR WAX BEANS

Wax beans too often taste pallid but these add a tart contrast to roast pork or pot roast. French-cut 1 lb. wax beans and boil until tender in not quite enough water to cover them. Drain the beans and reduce the liquid to about 1 cup. Dice fine and brown several strips of bacon, stir 1 T flour into the fat and then the bean liquid. Next add salt, pepper, and 2 T each of sugar and white vinegar or lemon juice. Use more sugar or vinegar as it pleases you. When thick, pour over the beans and heat well. Should you prefer these cold (they make an excellent side dish with broiled steak instead of the inevitable green salad), substitute 2 T butter for the bacon and chill thoroughly after they have been dressed.

༄ BEETS AND GREENS IN SOUR CREAM

Here the young savory greens count as much as the beets. Dig a few handfuls of very small beets and gather enough leaves so that when they are cooked there will be equal quantities. Boil the beets separately and skin them. Rinse the greens, do not dry them, discard the stems if tough, and cook slowly as you would spinach, adding a pinch of sugar, 2 T butter and a minced onion but no water. When they are tender, remove the cover and boil away as much of the juices as possible. Add the beets, chop quite fine, sprinkle with salt, pepper and 1 T lemon juice, heat through and just before removing from the fire stir in 2 or 3 T sour cream. Serve with a topping of grated egg yolk.

ॐ FRIED GREEN CABBAGE

A cooked cabbage should bear no resemblance to a discarded wig. This, properly prepared, is one of the gentlest and most delicate vegetables. Choose a summer cabbage that is light in weight, pale green in color, not too large or sullied by time. Cut the cabbage in quarters and soak ½ hour in salted ice water. Drain, shred coarsely, and steam in a very small amount of water with a pinch of caraway for 5 minutes, covered. Drain again, this time absolutely dry. Fry 1 medium minced onion, or 4 or 5 scallions chopped with their tops, in 4 T butter for a minute or so, only until it is palest gold. Stir in ½ t prepared mustard, add the cabbage, salt and pepper. Fry for only 5 minutes more. Add a few drops lemon juice and 2 T sour cream before serving. It must be served at once and the cabbage should be crisp, green and tenderly delicious.

ॐ CAULIFLOWER AND FRESH MUSHROOMS

Cauliflower, like cabbage, is usually ruined by overcooking. Take a young snowy head, leaving on some of the delicate inside leaves, and steam it whole in salted water reaching only to the top of the stalk—¼″ deep should be enough. Cook it only until it can be pierced lightly with a fork. Drain and keep dry on a platter in a warm oven. (Don't ever keep drained vegetables warm in a covered pot because the steam will only draw off more juices and make the vegetables soggy.) Meanwhile prepare ½ lb. whole mushrooms by fry-

ing them in butter, covered for 3 or 4 minutes and uncovered
for 3 or 4 more. Salt and pepper them, sprinkle with a few
drops of lemon juice and minced parsley, heap them around
the head of cauliflower; over all, pour a cup of cream sauce
in which you have melted just a little Swiss or Cheddar
cheese.

❧ BRAISED CELERY

With proper seasoning cooked celery, almost never served,
becomes exciting. Cut the stalks diagonally into 1″ pieces,
and now again the secret is not to overcook the celery but to
maintain its crispness and fresh flavor. Melt a large lump of
butter in a frying pan, add 1 chicken bouillon cube and
squash it with the back of a wooden spoon, add the celery
pieces and mix with it 1 T tomato paste or chili sauce and a
dash each (no more) of soy sauce and Worcestershire. Remember, however, that these seasonings are intended only
to heighten the flavor of the celery, not to conceal it. Add
pepper (the bouillon cube and soy sauce should supply
enough salt), stir often, and fry just until tender but still
firm. Thicken with cornstarch mixed with water, using only
enough to glaze the pieces lightly. This is good with chops.

❧ SHAVED CORN

It was with a shriek from Aunt Dell that I learned this recipe.
In the country, with nature so prodigal, one is always likely
to pick more sweet corn than one's guests can eat. One evening after supper, I was about to throw away half a dozen
leftover cooked ears when, with the above-mentioned shriek
of dismay, Aunt Dell exploded with the proper directions for
saving the poor kernels: *never* throw old corn away, she

moaned, like a discarded kernel herself. I have since learned that this is also an excellent way to utilize uncooked cobs when they have been left on the stalk past the stage of perfection, or even those small green cobs that inadvertently have been picked before they are quite ripe.

It is, though, a tedious job to shave the corn. Do it when you have those well-meaning guests around who keep asking if they can't help. Hand each a very sharp paring knife and put him to work hacking away at the cobs to cut off every last kernel of corn. For 6 ears of corn, melt 3 T butter in a skillet, add the shaved corn, 1 small minced onion, ¼ cup milk, ¼ green pepper and ¼ sweet red pepper (chopped), salt, 1 T parsley and fresh pepper. Cover and simmer slowly —Aunt Dell insists it must be at least an hour and she should know. This is a delicious way to prepare corn for the freezer.

ಶಿ KOHLRABI WITH GREENS

Kohlrabi has almost been forgotten (and understandably so, when one sees it in city markets, woody as a croquet ball and nearly as large, with an inglorious crown of wilted yellow leaves). But it is a beautiful vegetable if picked when no larger than a pullet egg, its leaves still green and tender. The skin should be paper-thin and pare easily. Slice the kohlrabi thin (it is wonderful for cocktails, too, sliced raw and salted) and cook 2 heaping cups in very little water. Pick out the young, furling leaves, chop them up, and cook them in about 1 cup water until very tender. Drain but save the liquor of both, reducing it to ¾ cup altogether. Melt 2 T butter, blend in 2 T flour, then the liquor and finally ¼ cup light cream. Add the sliced kohlrabi and the greens, which you have since chopped as fine as possible—they are lovely green islands in the sauce. Season with salt and fresh pepper and a splash of paprika or cayenne. Dust lightly with mild cheese if you like.

ஃ KOHLRABI AND NEW POTATOES IN CREAM

When the leaves toughen, though the root itself is still tender and not woody, I like kohlrabi this way. Slice it thin and cook in a little water and salt until just tender. Meanwhile boil about twice as many small new potatoes and skin them. Combine the two with enough rich cream sauce to cover them, 1 t celery seed, salt, pepper and a pinch of caraway. Lay several strips of bacon over the top, then a good layer of grated Parmesan cheese, and place in a very hot oven until the bacon is crisp.

ஃ LEAF LETTUCE IN CREAM

Wash the lettuce and drain it dry. Have it crisp and chilled. Mix ¼ cup sugar with ¼ cup white vinegar and stir into ¾ cup light sweet cream. Bathe the lettuce in this and let it stand 10 minutes before serving. Add no seasonings. not even salt or pepper, for the flavor of this delicate lettuce should be tampered with no further.

ஃ MARBLE POTATOES

I really mean marble-sized new potatoes. When potatoes are dug, there are always tiny ones, no larger than a hickory nut, clinging near the larger tubers and usually these are discarded. It is a pity. Wash them well and put them, if possible, into an iron pot. Turn the flame low and add almost no water at all; in fact, nearly burn them. Cover them and shake them often. When they are tender, remove the cover; when they are absolutely dry, add a generous lump of butter, douse well with salt and pepper, and add a smattering of green onion or chopped chives. Sizzle them uncovered for another minute. Gobble them whole, skins and all.

ONIONS IN BUTTER AND SHERRY

When the garden onions have grown to an inch in diameter, toss them into a skillet with a good supply of butter (use the drained, canned onions in other seasons). Add pepper, but no salt, and a little parsley. Heat through, and when the butter begins to brown add ½ cup light sherry. Cover, simmer without browning until the onions are tender, and pour this as a garnish over a broiled steak.

BAKED-STEWED FRESH TOMATOES

Remembering that she does not believe in fresh uncooked vegetables, I was not surprised to find this dish on Ruth Hummock's table one hot summer evening, though in her garden the bushes were laden with fat red globes waiting to be gulped raw. One spoonful, however, and I knew its virtue. Every aroma and taste of the earth remained, despite Ruth's highhanded scorn of them.

Dip 6 plump, ripe tomatoes in boiling water and peel them. Fry a thick slice of country bacon, or 2 ordinary slices, until crisp. Remove the bacon, cut the tomatoes into chunks and add to the remaining fat, add salt, pepper, 1 medium sliced onion, 2 t brown sugar, and seasoning of marjoram, basil, or fresh dill. Simmer until the tomatoes are barely tender. By no means let them get mushy. Add the crumbled bacon. Place in a casserole and if it is too watery, thicken slightly with cornstarch. Cover the top generously with buttered bread cut in cubes and bake in a hot oven until these are brown and crusty.

ॐ HERB-STUFFED TOMATOES

When the tomato vines begin to ripen in horrifying quantities, every country gardener must try to find new ways of utilizing them. This dish is wonderfully refreshing for lunch on a hot day. Peel the tomatoes after dipping them in boiling water, cut out the centers, squeeze out the seeds (be careful not to bruise or misshape the tomatoes) and chill them. Beat an egg along with 1 T each of flour and sugar, stir in ½ cup milk and cook until thick, stirring constantly. Add 1 T wine vinegar and pour the mixture over an 8 oz. package of cream cheese softened at room temperature. Add salt, pepper, a small grated sweet pickle, and a very liberal supply of fresh, finely minced herbs—basil and tarragon are wonderful, or dill, chervil or borage. Fill tomatoes with this mixture, top with chopped, hard-boiled egg. Chill again.

ॐ FRIED GREEN TOMATOES

Each summer I wage a battle to let the first tomato ripen to its destined redness, without consigning it while still green to the frying pan. I can restrain myself when I recollect that by the season's height there will be an ample supply of both ripe and unripened. Then I search the vines for firm, plump green tomatoes. These are cut into ½″ slices, dipped in milk, and then into flour with which I have mixed salt, pepper, and a little brown sugar or, better still, maple sugar. They should then be fried slowly, preferably in chicken fat or else in half-butter and half-vegetable shortening, until they are crisp, brown and tender. Some of my farm neighbors make a milk gravy of the juices and crumbs left in the pan, adding a bouillon cube for further flavor, and pour this over the fried tomatoes on toast. It's a very good lunch dish.

ह TOMATO AND SPINACH CASSEROLE

Prepare fresh or frozen spinach, chop it coarsely, sprinkle with lemon juice and 2 T sour cream, mix with it a can of button mushrooms browned in butter, and place in a casserole. On this, place several layers of sliced ripe tomatoes, each dusted with salt, pepper, and Parmesan cheese. Put a heavy layer of cheese on top, dot well with butter, and bake in a hot oven until browned. This is also fine with steak.

ह BROILED BABY ZUCCHINI

Consider the fat, cucumber-size zucchinis usually found in markets as monsters, and pick them when they are no more than three or four inches long and still slim. Do not peel them. Split them lengthwise and place in a buttered shallow pan. On each, put a little minced garlic, salt, fresh pepper, minced parsley or chives, a coating of grated Parmesan, and either a generous pat of butter or diced thick bacon. Place under a low broiler but not for too long. They should remain firm and rather crisp.

ह ZUCCHINI (OR CROOKNECK SQUASH) IN SOUR CREAM

If the squash are young enough (as they should be), do not peel them but cut them into thin slices. Melt 3 or 4 T butter and in it cook several minced scallions for a minute or two, but do not let them brown even slightly. Add the squash, salt, pepper, and cook over a low flame, covered, until it is tender, which won't be long. Watch that it does not burn and if necessary add more butter or a drop of water. Do not drain. Dress generously with sour cream, heat through, and after it is dished up, be lavish with a topping of chopped, fresh dill. The garden can supply few things more pleasing than this.

Some of the garden vegetables have special affinities for meats: carrots, onions and peas always belong with beef, it seems to me; or string beans with lamb; Swiss chard and cauliflower ask for ham or pork. Often the dawdling summer afternoon has been too relaxing—why did I have to pick up idly my old copy of *Sons and Lovers* or Sarah Orne Jewett's *Country of the Pointed Firs* this afternoon, just as I had myself all steamed up to weed the herb patch? Or sometimes summer callers have taken up too much time, even though pleasantly. Or a visit to a neighbor's pier for a short, cooling swim has somehow turned into an afternoon of talk and tall, cooling drinks instead. Then I find it convenient to remember these vegetable and meat affinities and, with a simple sauce, quickly prepare a one-dish meal for my casual supper. Of these, my favorites are:

ɞ SWISS CHARD WITH HAM

Cut the ribs from young, waving, deep-green fans of Swiss chard, dice them, and cook a few minutes in very little water. Drain the ribs and add the chard leaves which have been washed but not dried. Add a lump of butter, salt, pepper, but no water, and cook covered until done on low heat. Place in a shallow casserole and sprinkle with minced onion. Lay on this a slice of center-cut ham about ¼" thick. Make a sauce of 2 T butter, 2 T flour and ¾ cup milk or light cream. When thickened, stir into it ½ cup dry white wine and pour over the ham. Top it all with grated Parmesan cheese, a few bread crumbs and dots of butter. Bake ½ hour in a 350° oven or until the ham is tender. If necessary, run under the broiler to brown the top.

☙ CAULIFLOWER WITH HAM CASSEROLE

Steam (not quite done) a head of cauliflower in water just covering the stem. Put a slice of ham in a casserole. Break the cauliflower florets over this. Salt and pepper. Next pour over 1 cup light but well-seasoned white sauce. Cover the whole with very thin slices of really good, aged American cheese and place strips of bacon on top of this. Bake in a moderate oven ½ hour or more until the ham is tender, the cheese melted, the bacon crisp, and the whole brown and bubbly.

☙ LAMB STEW WITH GREEN BEANS

This, of course, is not for last-minute preparation. But when I know I am going to be busy all day, I cook it the night before or in the morning. Then when dinnertime comes, there it is, ready to be heated, and all the better for waiting.

Have several pounds of spring lamb cut into 1″ pieces. Brown these in butter or bacon fat, add salt, pepper, 1 t fresh or ½ t dried summer savory, ½ t peppercorns, and 1 cup water or ½ cup water and ½ cup light dry white wine (but it must be a light wine or its flavor will predominate). Cover and simmer very slowly until it is nearly done. A half-hour before it is ready, add 1 lb. fresh green beans, whole or French-cut, a diced potato, a handful of whole scallions, leaving on part of the greens, and more water if needed. Thicken the gravy with flour that has been browned golden either in the oven or on top the stove in a skillet, stirring it often. Serve with cottage cheese dumplings which are delicate and fluffy (see page 157) or thin noodles dressed with butter and a few T cottage cheese. This is a lovely stew for summer, for its flavor remains light and fresh.

One small corner of the garden is always reserved for herbs, such as the summer savory required in the lamb stew above. Only a yard-square patch is needed to supply a summer's herbs, save for parsley and the greatest of them all— fresh dill. For this there is never enough room.

I have even known visitors, first smelling the clear, pungent aroma of its proud heads, to offer to eat it on breakfast cereal. So can it beguile one. All herbs have their own urges to sidle alongside certain vegetables—a sprinkle of freshly cut chives will perk up fried eggplant; marjoram blends perfectly with broccoli; tarragon is a great asset to plain buttered cauliflower; and sweet basil is a crown to sliced ripe tomatoes. But none is so versatile or exciting as fresh dill. Dill for the dill crock, dill with sour cream for squashes or iced thick-sliced cucumbers, dill tossed lightly into cold soups, dill for vinegars or green salads; but above all, fresh dill generously flavoring a pot roast. This is one of the true glories of summertime.

₴ POT ROAST WITH FRESH DILL

Cook this as proudly as you would a peacock. Brown a fine 3 or 4 lb. chuck or tip sirloin pot roast in fresh bacon fat in a Dutch oven. Salt and pepper both sides, spread the top side lightly with prepared mustard, sprinkle with the juice of half a lemon and toss in the squeezed rind, and lay on the meat a bed of thin-sliced onion—1 large onion is sufficient. Now reverently place on this 5 or 6 whole heads of fresh dill. Add 1 bay leaf and a dozen each of whole peppercorns and whole allspice. Pour over ½ cup dry red wine but no water. A good pot roast should supply enough juices of its own; if not, add water later as needed. Cover tightly and simmer several hours until the roast is tender. When ready, thicken the gravy cautiously with flour; don't let it become heavy. Strain the gravy and into it drop several more finely chopped heads of dill. Don't serve mashed potatoes with this. The subtly aromatic gravy should grace only the meat, and be sure this is carved as respectfully as you would a rib roast of beef, not in chunks but in *thin*, across-the-grain slices. A few new potatoes are good with this, boiled, peeled and browned crisp in pure butter, and for a salad try

৯ TOMATO SALAD WITH SWEET BASIL

Peel and slice, not too thickly, really ripe tomatoes. Serve them either with a dressing of 3 T oil to 1 T wine vinegar, salt, freshly ground pepper and a little sugar, or with a generous masking of Edna's Mayonnaise (see page 178). In either case sprinkle over the salad fine shreds of fresh sweet basil, allowing at least 1 T for each tomato. It is startling how tomatoes and basil embrace each other.

And one more surprising and delicious use for fresh summer herbs is

৯ SPAGHETTI WITH FRESH BASIL OR SAGE

Once you have tried it you will find yourself using this dish increasingly as a substitute for potatoes with roasts, steak or chops. Spaghetti-and-sage is best with the heavier meats. Spaghetti-and-basil is best with those more delicate, such as chicken or young leg of veal. For either, boil a package of thin spaghetti but avoid overcooking: chew a strand after 10 minutes and if you're not quite certain whether it is done or not, it is. Rinse quickly with hot water and drain well. Turn into a warm bowl in which you have some melted butter, add salt, pepper, and either the chopped sage or basil, being generous with the basil but sparing with the sage. Toss. Serve grated Parmesan cheese with it if you wish, but I like it better plain.

The basil and sage for the above recipes must (unfortunately for those who do not own a garden) be absolutely fresh. The dried variety will not do. (They can be raised in a window sill pot, however.) But fresh dill is available in every market in July and August; the inhabitant of even the stuffiest city apartment, possessed of a single gas burner, can be as happy as I am with a dill pot roast. I repeat, when this is brought to table, when the taunting fragrance of the dill reaches your nostrils, this is the finest hour of the summer.

CHAPTER FOUR

CUKES BY THE GALORE

AND BEFORE *Anethum graveolens* vanishes from garden and markets (so evanescent it is, like all great things) I can be certain a huge, somewhat battered limousine will pull into the yard; for Aunt Dell thinks as highly of fresh dill as I do. Each year when the green-golden heads are shimmering on their feathery stalks and the cucumbers sprawl on their vines in the warm, dusty earth, she will appear laden with bunches of one and basketfuls of the other, as well as with old wooden crates filled with cauliflowers, peppers, onions, green beans and wax beans (as though my own garden will produce nothing of worth). But such is the way of a neighbor like Aunt Dell, and she stands there looking like Ceres, grinning productively, jabbing her big thumb toward the loaded car.

"C'mon, mister," she orders, grabbing a bulging bushel basket singlehanded, "cart this stuff into your house, see? I got cukes by the galore in the garden again this year, so I brung you a load. Brung some green beans too. We'll get you your dill crock started." She smiles triumphantly, like the primal force of this ritual (which she is). "Ainna?"

Then begins on this day and through the following weeks

of the summer's peak, a session of canning and pickling, of "putting up" chutneys, piccalillies and chowchows, and above all the making of the dill crock, which, since she first taught me, has become a summer's event of great and resounding magnitude.

The first summer Aunt Dell arrived, a look of mystery flashed in her eyes as she called out to me from the huge car. "You got a crock, mister? A good big one? Anyhow, I brought me one along," she said, pointing toward the rear seat on which sat a five-gallon earthenware crock. I saw it was half filled with green beans. She beamed enthusiastically. "I got me so many crocks, I said to myself you just drag one along up the hill."

I had seen her in the village only the day before and was told sonorously that she was about to "fix herself up the dill crock." Now all these gifts, the crock, the bunches of dill, the baskets and boxes of vegetables and the cheery anticipation were the result of my having asked what a dill crock was— and glad I am that I did. She ordered me to grab some of the baskets and march them into the kitchen. I marched, and Aunt Dell marched after me, and the wonderful event began. I was ordered to peel garlic, while she set pots of water up to boil, measured and flipped and dipped and scooped and dumped vegetables into the crock. The aroma of the dill bouquets filled the kitchen.

Everyone *needs* a dill crock. It is as indispensable as Aunt Dell hinted it would be, as integral a part of summer as fire-flies or shooting stars. You come in hot and parched from hauling weeds to the compost heap or mowing the lawn and there is the crock like a big, open, restorative fountain to dip into (you never seal up the vegetables in jars—that would be ungenerous), and fish out one of the cool, crunchy, dilly morsels of bean, onion or cauliflower. It is like the tub of pickles in old grocery stores, and what has such a look of solid comfort, or such a feel of everlasting providence, as a large earthenware crock sitting in one's kitchen? It is always there to plunge into elbow-deep, a safeguard against life's inconstancies, a reminder that some good things endure.

We serve bowls full of these miraculous vegetables for cocktails or on the supper table. And certain visiting friends have been caught at three in the morning, creaking from their beds to tiptoe to the dark kitchen, making a whispered splash as their fingers search frantically in the crock before a quick race back to bed with the stolen delight.

❧ THE DILL CROCK

Fill a great crock (leaving room for the vegetables, of course) with a brine made of 10 measures of water to ¾ measure of salt, adding if you wish a small dollop of vinegar, but no more than ¼ measure for each 10 measures of water. Now have a good supply of fresh dill on hand, toss in a few cloves of garlic, but be very modest with these, and then begin packing in the fresh vegetables with generous layers of the dill in between. Try any of the firm vegetables your garden offers. Strange and marvelous things happen to green string beans, for instance, if parboiled only 2 or 3 minutes ("just long enough to get the fuzz taste off," Aunt Dell commands) and then flung into the brine-filled crock. Nothing nicer could happen to any bean; after only a few days of dreamy floating in their pungent bath they will become an exciting delicacy. Wax beans are good too, or small raw onions or raw baby carrots. It's fun to experiment. Raw young whole pods of peas emerge sweet and crunchy, as do raw cauliflower florets or cucumber chunks or little-finger-size pickles. A handful of grape leaves will do no harm to the flavor of your dill crock either. Nor will a sprig of cherry leaves. And as far away from here as Martha's Vineyard in Massachusetts (haven't I said the discovery of Aunt Dell's dill crock was an event of resounding magnitude?) Katharine Cornell has been known to toss a peach or two into hers.

ළ DILL BEANS

Certain of these vegetables are always more popular than others at cocktail time and to insure a lasting supply I always make an extra small crock of each. Most favored is the green dill bean, particularly for use in making Dill Bean Roll-ups (see page 135) for teatime or for appetizers. Take about 2 lbs. fresh beans and proceed as above, remembering to parboil them briefly (this is the only vegetable requiring cooking first to make it palatable). But I repeat, not more than 2 or 3 minutes, or the beans will grow soggy in the brine. Keep the crock at room temperature and they should be ready in 3 or 4 days. If during hot weather a scum then forms on the brine, they may be stored by rinsing them, packing them in jars with fresh brine and either fresh or the old dill, and kept in the refrigerator.

ළ DILL ONIONS

These are perfect to accompany Martinis. Use the small pickling onion and 2 lbs. will be sufficient, for it will be an afternoon's work to peel that many, but worth it. Proceed and store as above, though it will take them longer to mature in the brine. Keep tasting each day and see. Once pickled, they will remain firm in the refrigerator for months (if you can keep them that long).

➷ DILL TOMATOES

Some say *these* are the best. Use small green tomatoes of the Tom Thumb or cherry variety and proceed as above. These also take a week or more to mature and grow tender. Narrow strips of sweet red pepper can be intermingled with them. Use lots of dill. I like a bowl of these with a cold roast.

Not only did Aunt Dell supply me with cukes by the galore, but also with various recipes for their preservation; and not only for *their* preservation but for that of everything growing under the sun. In summertime she becomes a great hoarder. Everything edible must be sealed in a jar, rescued from a withering death on the vine.

But her winter's reward is great. Her fruit cellar is an array of green and yellow and pumpkin-colored and rosy things destined to a life everlasting (unless you eat them) in glasses and bottles. There are pale golden Slippery Slims bathing among equally golden mustard seeds, and spicy, sweet-sour wax beans (both of which I had not tasted since childhood). There are deep purple conserves rich with nut meats and small jars of homemade capers; to make them, she simply soaks large, firm, green seeds of nasturtiums (from her flower border) in vinegar until they are tender. In that rich storehouse are also cherry dills to be eaten with Sauerbraten or dark brown stews, and slim bottles of green tomato catchup which I had never tasted before, and stewed blueberries and horse-radish pickles and this kind of pickle and that.

As she does with everything, Aunt Dell hands out her recipes by the big fistful. These are the ones I cherish most:

➷ SLIPPERY SLIMS

Use fat, ripe cucumbers. Peel a dozen of them, cut in half lengthwise, scrape out the seeds, and then cut into long sticks about ½" square. Salt and let stand overnight. Drain and dry and boil them in a syrup of 1 qt. cider vinegar, 1½ lb. white sugar and 1½ lb. brown sugar, 2 T mustard seeds, 1 T whole cloves, 1 T cassia buds, 1 t whole allspice, a pinch of ginger, and several sticks of cinnamon. Don't over-cook them: they should become transparent and glazed but still be crisp. Seal in jars, pouring over them the boiled-down syrup to cover and be sure that there is a piece of cinnamon in each jar. To some of the jars I add a jigger of sherry.

৯ SWEET-SOUR WAX BEANS (FOR PRESERVING)

Cut 2 lbs. wax beans into 1" diagonal pieces. Cover well with water, add salt to taste and boil until just barely tender. Drain, saving the liquor, add to it 1 cup white vinegar, ½ cup sugar, 1 t celery seed, a pinch of ginger, 1 t dried sum-mer savory or 1 T chopped fresh, and additional water if necessary so that there will be enough liquid to fill the jars. Boil, add the beans, boil up again and seal in jars. Add a small bay leaf to each jar. Serve this nearly forgotten delicacy with pork instead of apple sauce.

৯ GREEN TOMATO CATCHUP

This is a distinctive and interesting condiment. Slice 1 peck green tomatoes and 3 large onions, place them in layers in a crock sprinkling salt in between, and let stand for 24 hours. Drain. Put them into a large kettle (Aunt Dell's is black and fat and shiny as a witch's) and add 2 cups vinegar, 3½ cups brown sugar, 1 T salt, ½ T whole black pepper, ½ t each of allspice, ginger and cinnamon, and 3 T prepared mustard. Add ¾ cup pickling spices tied in a bag and boil it all for 2 hours. Strain through a sieve and bottle.

CRYSTALLIZED GREEN TOMATOES

Though these take time to make, they require little effort, and the result is a crisp tomato pickle with somewhat the consistency of water chestnuts. Cut 7 lbs. green tomatoes into 1/4" slices and soak them for 24 hours in a gallon of water and 3 cups of lime. Rinse them well and soak 12 hours more in plain water. Now soak them another 24 hours in 2 gallons of water and 2 oz. alum. Rinse again, and for this stretch, soak them 6 hours in 2 gallons of water to which you have added 2 oz. ginger. (To come out right on your sleeping schedule it's best to begin this whole business in the evening.) After the ginger bath the tomatoes must stand for 3 hours more in a syrup made of 5 lbs. sugar, 6 pints vinegar, and 1 t each of ground cloves, ground allspice and cinnamon. Then boil all together over low heat and, thank heavens, seal in jars.

CHERRY DILLS

Wash the pickles and pack in a stone crock between layers of fresh dill and cherry leaves; it's the combination of these two that gives the pickles their pleasing flavor. Pour over them a brine of 5 qts. water to 1 cup salt and let stand for 2 weeks. Rinse the pickles in clear water, cut into 1" chunks and pack in jars. For each quart jar make a syrup of 2 cups sugar, 1 cup vinegar and mixed spices tied in a bag. Boil and pour hot over the pickles.

PLUM AND NUT CONSERVE

For a conserve as lush and deep-hued as a summer twilight sky, cut up 5 lbs. of ripe blue plums, 1 lb. raisins, a cup of walnut meats and mix with 5 lbs. sugar and the juice and grated rind of 2 oranges. Let this stand overnight. In the

morning, cook until it thickens but don't let it become too
thick; about 50 minutes of boiling should do it. Ladle into
glasses and seal with paraffin.

ৡ HORSE-RADISH PICKLES

This is from Aunt Dell's collection of old recipes, inscribed
on tablet paper in an unmaidenly hand of jagged mountain
peaks and cramped valleys by a maiden aunt, now long de-
ceased. I quote it as it is written: "Put pickels in water over
Night and dry the mornings. Put lots dill, 2 red pepper, 1
tablspon black pepper kerns (this was first misspelled "corns"
but corrected—you can see the erasure), 2 bay leaves, 2
pieces horse radish large like a quarter, 1 onions for 18 quarts
pickels. Cook 6 quart water with 1 lb. salt 1 scant teaspon
alum 4 cup sider vinigar boilet all together. Put over pickels
colt."

Ecstatic spelling and syntax or no syntax, these are very
good. It is the pieces of horse-radish large like a quarter
that give them their distinctive zest.

Aunt Dell one day discovered the herbs in my garden.
"These here herbs," she said, pronouncing "herbs" with a
great gust of aitches, "we should do something tasty with 'em,
ainna? Got some empty bottles and a vinegar jug?" It had not
occurred to me before that one might make one's own herb
vinegars, but nothing is beyond the knowledge of Aunt Dell.
Under her guidance there began a session of plucking herbs
and imprisoning them with vinegar in an assortment of bottles and setting them in the sun to steep. Every variety was ex-
perimented with, singly or in combination, basil in white vinegar for a gentle salad, tarragon and thyme, orégano in a dark
wine vinegar for an Italian dressing. Best of all, however, is

❧ GARLIC DILL AND FRESH MINT VINEGAR

I know of no three flavors which, tempered by vinegar, blend together so wholeheartedly and yet subtly. Into a quart bottle of cider vinegar (not wine, which has its own decided flavor) drop a peeled clove or two of fresh garlic (never use garlic powder, which, to me, makes anything it touches taste rancid). Insert 3 or 4 whole stalks of fresh fragrant mint into the bottle, and then 2 heads of fresh dill. Allow to steep in a warm place for several weeks and you will have a delicious, fruity, salad vinegar.

It's not Aunt Dell and I alone who pickle and preserve away our summer days. In neighboring homes, large and small, householders are harvesting and shopping and simmering and sealing. From Andy at the country hotel has come a recipe for corn relish, which the women of his kitchen must concoct by the hundred-gallon, for it is present on the dinner table every Sunday noon in the cool dining hall, and a party of eight will like as not empty a pint jar. New residents in our neighborhood, too, recently moved out from cities, find themselves all unexpectedly remembering chowchows and conserves their mothers or more remote forebears used to make. Old cookbooks are searched, letters are written to ancient half-forgotten aunts in Maine or Montana or far countries, to learn exactly how it was they used to make the peach jam that always appeared on breakfast tables a quarter-century ago. Suddenly it is vital to know such things. The past is always nearer in the country.

From several such friends have come excellent old pickling recipes of English origin.

❧ CONNIE'S ENGLISH MUSTARD PICKLES

The neighbor who supplied this recipe of her grandmother's says these wonderful pickles absolutely will not be good unless Coleman's mustard is used. Cut up 2 stalks celery, 4 qts. small cucumbers, 1 large cauliflower, 4 green and 2 red sweet peppers. Mix with this 3 qts. peeled small pickling onions, cover with 1 pt. salt and let stand overnight. Drain well in the morning. Make the sauce by mixing together 12 T Coleman's mustard, 2 T turmeric, 2 T curry powder, 4 cups sugar and 1 cup flour. Add enough cider vinegar to make 4 quarts. Cook until thick, pour over the vegetables and let come to the boiling point again but do not boil (as this would make the pickles soft). Seal in jars.

❧ CONNIE'S ENGLISH PICKLE SLICES

Slice 30 medium cucumbers as thin as possible. To them add 8 large chopped onions, 1 each green and sweet red pepper, chopped, cover with ½ cup salt, let stand 3 hours and drain. In a large kettle combine 5 cups cider vinegar, 5 cups sugar, 2 T mustard seed, 1 t turmeric and ½ t powdered cloves. Bring to a boil and add the pickles. Again, heat them thoroughly but do not let them boil. Seal at once.

❧ ENGLISH CHOWCHOW

Into a stone crock, sprinkling salt between them lightly, put a quart of young, tiny cucumbers not over 2″ long, 2 qts. small white onions, 2 qts. tender green beans cut in half, 2 qts. green tomatoes, sliced and coarsely chopped, 2 small fresh heads of cauliflower cut into pieces, and 1 small coarsely chopped head of cabbage. Let stand 24 hours and drain. Put into a large kettle with 1 oz. turmeric, 6 chopped red peppers, 4 T mustard seed, 2 T each of celery seed, whole cloves and whole allspice, 1 cup sugar and 6 T mustard, and enough cider vinegar to cover. Cover tightly, simmer, watch and stir, until all the vegetables are cooked through and tender. Seal hot. This superior chowchow grows even more superior as it ages.

֍ MAJESTIC HOTEL CORN RELISH

This should be made at the height of the corn season, of course, though at other times the frozen variety may be used. Boil 24 cobs of corn and cut the kernels from the ears. To this add 1 bunch celery cut very fine, 4 large onions and 2 each of green and red peppers put through the food chopper, 3 cups brown sugar, 3 cups vinegar, 2 jars prepared yellow mustard, 2½ t dry mustard, 2 T flour and salt to taste. Boil about ½ hour and seal hot.

Also, in Mrs. Brubaker's mammoth kitchen, the cool summer mornings will find her companionable chef Eugene busy over copper kettles making *his* special preserves. His, befitting Mrs. Brubaker's lavish table, are the spiciest, richest of all.

֍ BROWN SUGAR PEACHES IN PORT
OR BRANDY

Eugene uses fresh peaches that are slightly underripe. For 6 qts. peaches make a syrup of 3 lbs. brown sugar, 1 qt. cider vinegar, 2 cups water, 1 sliced lemon, 3 T whole cloves, 4 sticks cinnamon and a small piece of ginger. Boil the syrup until clear and add the peaches a quart at a time, cooking until heated through or about 5 minutes. Pack into jars, pouring 2 oz. of good brandy or port into each quart jar. When all the peaches are cooked, boil down the syrup slightly and pour hot over the peaches and seal at once. When these spicy peaches are served, Eugene never pours the syrup away: a good cook learns to hoard these small treasures. He uses it to marinate a mushroom salad (see page 51) or mixed with mayonnaise for a fruit salad or dribbled over iced fresh fruits for dessert. It is equally good to flavor a rum drink or a barbecue sauce.

ஃ CHERRIES IN CURRANT JELLY

Use the huge black canned Bing cherries for this. Strain them, saving the juice. Cook enough fresh ripe currants with a little water to make 3 cups of juice when pressed through a strainer. Add ½ cup of the black cherry juice and ½ cup claret. Bring to a boil, add 4 cups sugar and 2 cups of the strained cherries and cook slowly for about 10 minutes until it thickens. This will make poultry or game taste even better.

It was Eugene who made a sound observation while stirring a thick, fruity jelly over his range. Mrs. Brubaker was in the kitchen too, lured there by the winey aroma. People, Eugene said, don't can nearly enough any more, contenting themselves with spiceless commercial pickles and preserves, when anyone with the simplest kitchen equipment can put up a few jars of something against the drab, frantic winter. It's a wonderful comfort to have even a small remembrance of summer locked in a half-pint jar, stored away on your pantry shelf. I saw Mrs. Brubaker smile and nod.

Eugene is always right. And it was a proper time to be thinking of such things as trying to stash away a small memento of the summertime's pleasures. On the way home, on my hillside, I saw that the first branch of sumac had turned to flame.

CHAPTER FIVE

THE WILD FRUITS RIPEN

IN THE WOODS, along fence rows, in the hollows, something has been happening that never ceases to astonish me. In spring the wild plum trees had been frothy with blossom, while at their feet wild raspberries and blackberries cascaded more white bloom. The mulberry trees bloomed with their odd musky scent, wild currants had borne creamy clusters even while frost still stunned the night air, and the fragrance of flowering wild grape had made me heady. All this had seemed enough for anyone to ask of nature.

But then these same bushes and trees had, during the summer months, further busied themselves with producing fruit, unasked, unaided. Friends with pails tied to their belts had swarmed the woods in July, returning with raspberries, warm and sweet, and later with tart blackberries. These should be eaten, not in the usual way with sugar and sweet cream, but as Matt Barker pensively eats them—doused with sour cream and sprinkled with dark brown sugar. Before that, Rosalie Barker had come up one afternoon to ask whether she might pick the *green* currants along the fence—for pie, she said and smiled. Now each year as August ends its stint, the wild plums ripen; grapes tangling up the hills, sweetened by sun and wind, turn dusty purple for wines and conserves; in the woods the bright red chokecherries drip from the trees, ready to produce a marvelous, little-known jelly. And it's all free. How not be astonished by such rich gifts from the land?

Only a few years ago an aunt came to visit me. Though now she lives in Toledo, Aunt Elsa had been born not far from here, sixty-odd years ago, among these woody hills. She had not been back, however, since her marriage. Now she was widowed. She sat on the terrace one late afternoon, and I could detect a restlessness about her while she mended a month's supply of my socks. (She is not a rustic aunt, however; she holds her own at scrabble and canasta, drinks Planter's Punch and drives a Chrysler convertible.) Her narrow face is lined, her hair the color of iron, her eyes seem to see far and starkly away. Suddenly she gave me a queer, rather desperate smile. For her, her voice sounded small.

"Let's go look for the mulberries. It's about time."

"What mulberries?"

"Near where Grandpa's farm used to be. We always used to picnic under the trees. I think I remember where they were. And when they were ripe, Ma made wonderful pies."

We set out in the Chrysler on a strange journey. She usually drives with zest and purpose, but now we crawled, loitering at this crossroads—"I think it used to be this way. . . ." Then, dawdling near the crumbles of a fieldstone barn: "that must have been the old Timm barn, so they should be near here someplace. . . ." Since she had last traveled here as a young woman, much had changed: old dirt roads abandoned, new highways built where there had been swamps, my grandfather's land itself requisitioned by the state, the buildings torn down, the lovely acres made part of a State Kettle Moraine Park and game preserve.

Aunt Elsa squinted, seeming to be lost in painful remembering, and swerved abruptly through a clump of hazel thicket only to discover an ancient roadway I had not even known existed. She drove slowly, steadily, silently. I thought I could feel her tremble as she searched so fearfully for the past. I could not help but wonder what young girl rode beside me, what plain or fancy dress she wore, what boy she thought about, boldly or diffidently, what she carried in her picnic basket. It must have been a wagon she rode in, of course. I felt the joggling. Then an even younger girl was racing beside us, laughing, shouting long-forgotten phrases to parents sitting on the high wooden seat.

She turned again, down another unknown road, picking up speed a little as if in impatience. A light came into her eyes. She laughed, in not quite a laugh. "Of course, even if I find the place, the trees won't be there any more."

We passed a tamarack swamp and began to climb a hill. Neither farmhouse nor barn was in sight. Dust rose behind us and locked out today. Then all at once Aunt Elsa stopped the car. She did not have to tell me. There they stood, a cluster of seven or eight in a sort of clearing on the hilltop under an effulgent sky; and they were heavily drooping with knobby, long, glistening mulberries, some pale green, some ruby, some jet. The trees had been waiting all this time.

A few were dead, a few were only newlings. While we gathered a whole pailful of the berries, Aunt Elsa told me with darting eyes how often she had visited the mulberry grove with her mother, who had spread a worn white sheet on the grass beneath the trees, then had gently shaken the branches, while both had stood together watching the fat, juicy berries plop down.

"And wait till you taste the pie," she said as we walked back to the car, but now she was excited and cheerful. "I think I remember how Ma made it."

The pie that night for supper was indeed worth our afternoon's search, with a gentle wildness in its filling that I've never tasted in pies made with cultivated fruits. Aunt Elsa said her mother often made another kind of pie, equally good, using ripe elderberries. There were other wild-fruit recipes she then recalled, which have since become staples of our summertime.

୫ MULBERRY PIE

Drive into the country some sunny Sunday and search along neglected roadways for wild mulberries or lush, ripe elderberries. For the mulberry pie, line a tin with a good, flaky crust. Fill with ripe mulberries and, since their flavor is somewhat bland, sprinkle over the juice of half a lemon. Next comes 1 cup sugar and the slightest dusting of nutmeg or mace. Cover with a second crust, sealing the edges well, and bake 35 minutes in a 400° oven.

୫ ELDERBERRY AND APPLE PIE

Ripe elderberries can sometimes be found at farmers' markets. Strip the washed berries from their stems (a wide-toothed comb is good to use) until you have a cupful. Fill a pastry shell nearly full with sliced tart apples. Sprinkle the elderberries over this and top with 1½ cups sugar. Cover with another crust and bake as you would any apple pie. The fruity tang of the elderberries in this pie makes it worth while to hunt for them.

ওৈ BLACKBERRY ROLL

This favorite of my grandmother's has become a summer favorite of mine with afternoon coffee or iced tea, though it is equally good for dessert. Mix together 2 cups flour, ½ t salt, 4 t baking powder, and cut in 4 T shortening. Lightly mix in 1 cup grated, good American cheese and then ⅓ cup milk. Roll the dough lightly to ⅓″ thickness and spread on it 2½ cups blackberries mixed with ½ cup granulated sugar and a generous ¼ cup brown sugar. Roll up like a jelly roll and bake about 45 minutes in a moderate oven or until golden. This is good either hot or cold and I like it especially when each slice is topped with 1 t sour cream.

ওৈ SPICED WILD GOOSEBERRIES

Pick the gooseberries when they are not quite ripe. For 6 lbs. stemmed berries, boil up 8 cups sugar, 2 cups cider vinegar, 1 T ground cinnamon, 1 t each of ground cloves and allspice, ½ grated nutmeg and ½ cup homemade sweet elderberry or dandelion wine (I use domestic port). Thicken slightly, add the berries and cook until it jells. With cold meats, there is nothing better. My grandfather, I'm told, ate a jar at a meal with disastrous and inevitable results.

ওৈ DAMPFNUDEL WITH STEWED FRUIT

These dumplings, Aunt Elsa remembers, were served with any stewed wild fruits, but especially with raspberries (or in wintertime with prunes). It is a pleasing light dessert but my grandmother always ate it for noon dinner—that is, it *was* her dinner. Mix together 2 cups flour, 2 beaten eggs, 1 t sugar, 1 t salt and 1 cup tepid milk into a few spoonfuls of which ½ oz. yeast has been dissolved. Knead the dough, let it rise, and with floured hands shape lightly into round dumplings.

Cover these and let rise again in a warm place. Next drop the dampfnudel carefully into a kettle of salted boiling water or milk; steam them gently about 15 minutes, closely covered, until they are done. They should be spongy and light and not the least bit moist. Drain them well and carefully, and serve covered with brown butter and a side dish of stewed fresh berries with lots of juice. The berries may be poured right over the buttered dampfnudel if you prefer.

੩ FLOWER HONEY
This recipe of my grandmother's makes me feel a deep abiding affection for her memory. Pick 6 red clovers, 30 white clovers, and 4 full blown roses. Boil 5 cups sugar with 1¼ cups water and 1 level t alum for a minute or until it is clear. Pour over the flowers, let stand 10 minutes and bottle. It should be fun to try on a fine summer's day.

੩ GREEN CURRANT PIE
Rosalie Barker is also skillful in using the fruits of the woods and fields, and this pie is another startling breakfast favorite of her husband's. Pick a quart of currants while they are still mostly green and just a few of them are beginning to ripen. Stem the currants and mix them together with 1½ cups sugar, a pinch of cinnamon, and 2 T flour. Bake as a two-crust pie in a moderately hot oven and wonder why you've never tried this before.

Then come the blueberries.

I have an odd passion for them, perhaps because when I was a child, on fishing expeditions to northern Wisconsin, one afternoon was always reserved for Blueberry Picking. There, in the wild, dry, scrubby fields they grew plentifully and supplied a winter's hoard of jams and preserves. I think it is the picking itself I recall more than the taste—the clean, hot sun on your stooped back, the sharp drift of wintergreen in your nostrils as you stepped on that creeping plant in error, the silence of the north, my father's sudden shout of "Look, sonny, a buck!" though I never glimpsed one. . . .

No sooner had I settled out here than my eyes fell on an illustration of magnificent, cultivated blueberry bushes in a plant catalogue. They need to be grown in sets of four, the catalogue said, of various species and sexes; twenty dollars for the set of four and each bush would produce a truckload. It seemed the happiest twenty dollars I had ever spent. That first summer I exuberantly also planted Florence fennel, artichokes, both globe and Jerusalem, peanuts, black-eyed peas and French endive. With forty acres of land, enthusiasm and plenty of time, why not? And what human being, newly moved from town to country fields yawning with promise, has not done the same? The weeks stretched into a season, I strained my eyes, and never has land remained so barren.

The blueberries, however, seemed to prosper; at any rate, they did not die, and the following spring produced a new set of shiny green, if small, leaves. After several years of outrageous attendance upon them, including bedding them down with straw each November, one summer there finally appeared a blueberry, one, the size of a plum, not very tasty. At which, whether in triumph or distress, all four plants promptly died.

But a friend who still vacations up north returns each summer with wooden pailfuls of the wild berries. The fields must still produce as extravagantly as they did years ago. With these she bakes a cake and makes a preserve that are worth the back-breaking effort of picking. But I am not too envious.

I have found the cultivated berries just as good to use, if you don't buy the monster-sized ones, grown for vain appearance rather than flavor. Choose those that *look* like blueberries, humble and openhearted.

৯ BLUEBERRY CAKE

If you buy the berries, my friend says, buy two boxes—one for the children to pilfer. Beat an egg well, and stir it vigorously into 5 T shortening creamed with ½ cup each of white and brown sugar. Sift together 1¾ cups flour, 2 t baking powder and ¼ t salt and add to the mixture alternately with ¾ cup milk, starting and stopping with the flour. Toss in ¼ t grated lemon peel and ½ t lemon extract, beat well; lastly, fold in a cup of fresh blueberries very gently. Bake in a 9″ square pan, lightly greased, in a 350° oven for about ½ hour. Serve this warm under a slab of ice cream.

৯ BLUEBERRY PICKLE

There is nothing more complicated to this than to fill glasses with plump, firm blueberries, having first sprinkled them lightly with a little grated lemon rind and ground cloves; add a stick of cinnamon and then pour into the glasses a light molasses, being sure it trickles into all the spaces. Cover only with pieces of cloth for these will spoil if sealed airtight. Set away, and soon the pickle will be sharp and delicious with heavy meats.

But most of all I wait for the wild plums to ripen. They grow in a small hollow in my woods and I watch their progress avidly. For once, I want to get to them before the birds do. When the small fruits have finally turned deep red and tender, and I pick them in the fading, cooling light of afternoon, it means I can go home with my bounty to prepare one of my favorite dishes:

ぞ VEAL WITH WILD PLUMS

The wild plums supply a unique tartness of their own; but I have found that when they are not available, preserved green gage plums, commercial beach plum jelly or even black currant jelly make pleasing substitutes. Lard a veal roast well with butter and chicken fat or strips of bacon, lay on top of it a good handful of celery tops, sprinkle with the juice of half a lemon and add a large bay leaf, salt, and a dozen each whole allspice and peppercorns. Baste often while the veal roasts in a moderate oven, adding a little water if necessary. A half hour before the meat is done, add a good cupful of wild plums to the pan, or ½ cup of the jellies mentioned. Also add ¾ cup water. When ready to serve, remove the celery tops and the roast (the celery will be brown and crisp and good for a garnish) and rub the remainder of the contents of the pan through a sieve to get a smooth, rich sauce. Taste it; sometimes I find it needs a little brown sugar and/or ½ t prepared mustard. Or I add 1 t capers. Simmer for a few minutes gently and don't let it burn. This sauce should need no thickening. If it does, use cornstarch, not flour. And this is not a sauce for mashed potatoes. Wild rice is good with it.

Eating this, savoring the untamable spirit the plum has harbored inside its thin skin (the first plum on earth must have tasted this way, wild and sharp), I always experience a further awareness of fall to come, of vigor reawakening after summer's inertia, of the peculiar, urging restlessness and final calm that autumn always brings.

CHAPTER SIX

THE CHEESE CROCK

THERE ARE MANY THINGS you should be doing as summer wanes: the woods paths need clearing, bulbs must be ordered, the three-feet-in-diameter slabs of the great, lightning-struck elm are still waiting to be laid for the new shade terrace (the elm is so stone hard they should last forever), the obscene tomato worms are ravishing the tomato vines and should be annihilated. But a slumberous quality has crept into the air, a faint, fearless sense of things drawing near their completion. From a neighbor's field a reaper whines as it cuts the harvest. You had not known it was that late.

On such afternoons it is more reasonable to dabble mildly about the yard and—say, around three o'clock—knock off the day's work, though it may have begun only half an hour before. It's a time for drowsing in the shade or, if you're with friends, sipping a tall drink, the talk laconic. You reflect and debate peaceably on matters of great importance: whether the old country remedy of wet mud would really cure a wasp sting, whether the pin oak is a lovelier tree than the white oak, and whether it really endangers the character of city people never to have had the chance to stretch their naked toes in cool, dry grass.

The drink for these occasions is called House on the Hill. It was invented because a friend gave me a bottle of Amer Picon. (Not knowing what else to do with it, I hazarded several experiments; the result of one was more than exhilarating.) The house I built is also called the House on the Hill, not through any choice of mine but because my Welsh neighbors simply began calling it that. The Welsh do that. They call their neighbors the Man with the Apple Trees; or someone's farm is called the Valley with Rocks. I didn't know the name of my own place until one day in the grocery store a smiling farmer asked, "Well, how's things up at Y Ty a'r y Bryn?" I asked where that was. "Don't you know your own place? Y Ty a'r y Bryn?" The House on the Hill. The name was handed to me without choice, and it's been called that ever since.

In the same way the drink was christened without plan or will. I had, with the pride of any inventor, mixed one several times before for friends who stopped in. One afternoon Chappie Wolf was over, helping me replace some rotted fence posts. Around three o'clock I suggested knocking off work to have a drink—we'd been sweating along the fence row for nearly an hour anyway. Chappie glanced dubiously toward the sun but I asked quickly what he'd like. He scratched his head. "Well, what about one of those House on the Hill's?" he said offhand.

The name stuck, and fits.

৯ HOUSE ON THE HILL COCKTAIL

In a tall glass pour 1½ jiggers Amer Picon, 1½ jiggers dry gin, ½ jigger crème de cacao. Fill the glass with shaved ice, and then pour in as much strong black coffee, previously chilled, as the glass will hold. A T of cream floated on top is

optional. For a midafternoon drink, serve cucumber sandwiches with this—the cucumbers sliced thin, unpeeled, generously salted and peppered, and put between thin slices of
pumpernickel. This drink is best taken in a hammock, and
one is plenty. As you drain the glass the House at which you
gaze grows more beautiful, the Hill on which it rests mounts
to a precipice, and it's time for a nap.

Summer naps in the country are apt to be of short dura-
tion, however, because you'll probably soon be waked up by
friends dropping by for a cocktail on the cooling terrace. This
is the shining hour. It is a pity our cities have not succumbed
to the ritual of sidewalk-café-sitting, for a cocktail sipped in
fresh air seems much less dangerous than one gulped in a
neon bar, where you never know what time of day it is. Outdoors, there are things to absorb your attention—clouds, birds,
the first leaf falling, a neighbor's cows lolling homeward in
the distance, or a train passing behind the hills, and you don't
drink so fast or so desperately.

I like a long cocktail hour (and so do my friends, I hope)
with only a small group, so there will be good talk rather than
words exchanged on the run. I relish these few captive hours
when life will do your bidding. The talk rises excitedly and
suddenly falls to a gentle lull, like the evening breeze. A fire-
fly is passing by. The lingering summer dusks are made for
pleasant talk and Martinis or Daiquiris and shrimps in dill
sauce and raw kohlrabi sliced paper-thin and salted and strewn
with freshly ground pepper. But there must be adequate food
provision to span the long wait until dinner, or guests are
likely to drift away in body and spirit. Respectable appetizers
will help to prevent it.

But no soggy, disconsolate-looking canapés are ever

served, or glutinous dips dribbling from potato chips. Instead there is always the Cheese Crock and a supply of homemade Melba toast and thin-sliced, strong rye bread. The crock has by now become an institution in the homes of all my friends and neighbors. It is a solid pivot, omnipresent during cocktails, like a constable of the night ever ready to help steady the unsteady. Halfway through the exhilarating, talky, laughing, drinking session, other sustaining dishes appear, such as shrimps in dill sauce, which are especially delicious on hot nights, and homemade cheese wafers or dill bean roll-ups. All of these are approved with gusto by the men as well as the ladies.

৯৯ THE CHEESE CROCK

This is an endless pleasure to make because experiment and invention are necessary ingredients, and each man becomes master of his own special crock. Even the least imaginative cook fancies himself becoming an Escoffier while he dabbles away. A pound of sharp, aged Cheddar should be grated, and to it added 1 small package cream cheese and enough good olive oil to make a thick paste; pound away at it in a wooden bowl until it is of a velvety spreading consistency. Now add 1 t or so of dry mustard, a few caraway seeds if you wish, and a few jiggers of brandy or wine or both—this is where your own talents come into play. Brandy and kirsch are a fine combination, or bourbon and port, or just Madeira. Let your imagination carry you away.

The fun from now on is that whenever you have a piece of cheese left around the house, you grate it into the crock; the last drops left in wine or liqueur bottles meet a similar end. Some of the old cheese should always be saved to act as the "mother" when you renew the crock. A variety of cheeses may be used. Roquefort is good, used sparingly. Keep the cheese spread in the icebox in a covered stoneware crock; take out an hour before using, and serve right in the crock with a few hefty spreading knives.

৯ SHRIMPS AND DILL SAUCE

Here again the ever-accommodating fresh dill blends tauntingly with the shrimp. Boil as many shrimps as are needed until they are tender in water to which 1 t caraway seed has been added. Peel and chill. Then make whatever amount of sauce is required as follows, allowing 1 cup sauce for each pound of frozen shrimps:

Mix equal parts of homemade mayonnaise (see page 63) and hollandaise sauce, which has been allowed to cool. If desired, the hollandaise may be omitted, using instead all homemade mayonnaise with 1 heaping T sour cream whipped with a fork into each cup of mayonnaise. Add a dash of cayenne. For each cup of sauce, add 2 large heads of finely chopped fresh dill and 1 t capers. Chill, and an hour before serving whip the sauce gently with a fork. Heap lavishly over the shrimps on a deep platter and sprinkle generously with more chopped dill. Garnish with thin-sliced tomatoes from which the seeds and juice have been squeezed before slicing, parsley, and a good supply of tiny pickled onions.

৯ HOLLANDAISE SAUCE

I include this because hollandaise is too often bemoaned as tricky to prepare. It is no such thing. This sure-fire recipe requires no boring, endless stirring in a double boiler, no adding of butter bit by bit. And it won't curdle. I prepare it in one minute flat and few sauces could be simpler to make.

Melt ¼ lb. butter in a saucepan. Remove from flame and
add the strained juice of ½ lemon or more to taste, a pinch
of salt, 3 egg yolks, and 1 T light cream or water. Mix well
and return to a medium flame, stirring the sauce constantly
with a wooden spoon or wire whisk until of the desired consistency. If it should be too thick, add a little more cream or
hot water. If not thick enough, add another egg yolk. I often
prepare this sauce in advance, and simply reheat it at the last
moment if it is needed to serve over vegetables, for instance.

੬ CHEESE WAFERS

Mix together 1 cup flour and 1¼ cups grated sharp Cheddar
cheese. Cut into this ¼ lb. butter as you would for any pie
dough. Roll the dough into a long sausage about the thickness of a quarter, wrap in wax paper and chill several hours in
the refrigerator; the dough will, for that matter, keep for a
week or two. When needed, slice off the wafers thinly, as you
would icebox cookies, and bake in a moderate oven on a
lightly greased cookie sheet until golden tan, about 10 minutes. These are delicious. For variation I sometimes add 1 or
2 T minced ham to the dough, or 1 T finely chopped parsley
or chives. Or the wafers may be sprinkled with caraway or celery seed before baking.

੬ DILL BEAN ROLL UPS

The method for preparing the dill beans is described in an
earlier chapter. (See page 112.) Trim the crusts from slices of
soft white bread, spread very thinly with mayonnaise, and
place on each a dill bean. Sprinkle with freshly ground pepper, and roll up the bread slice. Wrap in wax paper and place
for an hour or two in the refrigerator. When wanted, cut
each roll into half or thirds; keep them a husky size, which

the men will appreciate. Brush all over with melted butter and broil until golden, turning them to brown on both sides. Long, quartered sticks of dill pickle may be substituted for the dill beans, though they are not so good. If I must use pickles, I also add a sliver of ham.

The winey talk goes on and on. Sometimes, with other subjects exhausted (such as local taxes or a recent barn fire or the advisability of trying to raise sheep), the talk turns not unnaturally to food. Hank tells how his mother used to bake potato pancakes in the oven, dotted with salt pork; Joe tells about wild Canadian goose in bourbon though his wife Mary argues it should be brandy. By now it's all one with Joe and he says just leave out the cherries and bitters, that's all. Country people transplanted from cities enjoy talking about food almost endlessly, since they have discovered the delight (and turmoil and despair) of growing their own vegetables. But sometimes the talk gets out of hand, and turns to planning menus for a dinner for People You Can't Stand, with a main course of Wieners Stuffed with Peanut Butter in Lime Jell-o.

Then it is time for something more solid to restore and calm the drinkers until dinner—when *is* dinnertime, anyway, in the country? This is the moment to serve an Onion Pie, rich and filling. The joy of all these appetizers is that if they have been in ample supply, and the cocktail hour lasts long enough, you really needn't bother about dinner at all.

&~ ONION PIE
Mix together a dough of 1 cup flour, ¼ lb. butter, 2 T milk, and a pinch each of salt and sugar. Form into a ball and chill until it is easily handled. Roll out to fit an 8″ pie tin. Bake

10 minutes in a moderate oven, but be sure you have pricked the crust all over with a fork, or you are likely to end up with a tent.

For the filling, fry 4 strips of finely diced bacon until done. Drain, and in the bacon fat cook, until they are transparent, 2 large onions that have been diced *very* fine. Drain off fat, and mix bacon and onions with 1 egg and 1 egg yolk, previously beaten, a scant ½ cup sour cream, salt and pepper, some chopped chives and a sprinkling of caraway seeds. Pour into crust and bake at 350° until the filling is firm, about 20 or 25 minutes. This should be eaten warm, cut into narrow wedges that can be taken up with the hand.

ࣟ SPECKKUCHEN

A less rich and more doughy variation of the above. This time-honored Bacon Cake was relished by the old German burgher, not with cocktails, which he did not know existed and would have scorned, but as an honored observance around ten o'clock in the evening, either at home, interrupting his game of skat, or at his Stammtisch in the Bierstube— to stimulate his thirst and thereby stretch his capacity for beer. For the very same reason Speckkuchen has proved wonderful to serve at a beer picnic, held in the woods out here on any sultry Sunday afternoon.

Use any basic yeast dough that is not too sweet. Spread the dough in a thin layer in a medium-sized, oblong, buttered coffeecake tin. On the dough spread a thick layer of about ½ lb. fat bacon cut into small cubes. Over this, sprinkle 3 T chopped onions. Beat 3 whole eggs to a froth, stir in 1 heaping t caraway seed, and a liberal dose of salt and pepper. Spread this mixture over the bacon and bake in a hot oven for ½ hour.

Imperceptibly, the days shorten. You and your friends are sitting on the terrace, sipping Old Fashioneds because somehow, without even thinking much about it, the time didn't seem right for Daiquiris or Martinis, when a sudden chill brushes up the long meadow. At the edge of the woods you can see a thin hovering strip of mist. There is a peculiar silence; one of the girls laughs softly and asks for her cardigan, but instead of anyone going in after it we all rise and move into the house. You light the fire—it's time. Autumn has begun before you quite expected. You pull chairs close around the blazing apple boughs and sumac, which make the best fires, and soon the talk is noisy and cheerful again. On a table in the center of the group is the chafing dish. Nothing is more savory, these cooling evenings, than Swedish meatballs with chicken livers and mushrooms, simmering in wine in their copper pan over a faint blue flame.

ɞ SWEDISH MEATBALLS IN CHAFING DISH

This dish can be prepared before cocktail time. Ask the butcher to grind together three times ½ lb. round steak, ¼ lb. veal and ¼ lb. pork. Rub together with a wooden spoon until the meat mixture is very fine, slowly adding to it a piece of white bread, bit by bit, and a T or two of cream. Also mix in salt, pepper, a touch of ground allspice, and ¼ t nutmeg. Shape into very small balls, dust with flour, and brown gently in fresh bacon fat. Add as little water as will prevent them from burning, cover, and simmer as slowly as possible for about 20 minutes. Separately brown ½ lb. chicken livers in butter. Also cook in butter ½ lb. halved mushroom caps for 5 minutes. Salt lightly.

Put meatballs, livers and mushrooms, with their juices, in

the chafing dish. When ready to serve, add ¼ cup dry red wine and simmer all together for 10 minutes. Just before serving, stir in ½ cup sour cream.

Nothing more is needed for a casual buffet afterward than a rare roast beef, cooked previously and cooled at room temperature but not in the refrigerator, served sliced very thin, with well-buttered rye bread or pumpernickel and a brimming bowl of olives in oil. Lots of hot coffee later.

ह OLIVES IN OIL

Drain an assortment of large black, green, mottled and stuffed olives and marinate them for at least 1 hour at room temperature in 1 cup olive oil, 3 T wine vinegar, and a minced clove of garlic. The marinade should cover the olives and they should be stirred from time to time.

And much, much later, for those guests who have lingered on to watch the pale green September dawn spread behind the hills, it will be a kindness to prepare a healing and nourishing Cheese Soup.

ह CHEESE SOUP

For such occasions, it is wise to have on hand either a strong veal or chicken broth, cooked with a double dose of celery stalks and leaves, or a stock made of 4 chicken bouillon cubes to 4 cups water, simmered for ½ hour with a sliced carrot, 2 sliced onions, 3 large stalks of celery with leaves, and 1 bay leaf. Strain and store. For each portion, melt 1 heaping T of cheese from your cheese crock. Slowly stir into it ¾ cup of the strong broth and when boiling add ¼ cup light cream into which an egg yolk has been mixed. Heat only, and serve with lots of oyster crackers.

This is a soothing soup that will help you and your friends to a sound rest; you'll sleep in peace while a rising wind blows the last of summer away.

PART THREE

AUTUMN
CALM

CHAPTER ONE

AUTUMN FIRES

THE SUMMER PEOPLE have gone. The land has returned to its rightful owners: the farmer and year-round villager. This is the season of wind and rain, alternating with the smoke of last summer's leaves. A calm settles, of chores soon ending, a hint of the drowsy reward that winter will bring. At first as autumn begins, you want to run from this silence back to the loud safety of cities; then you accept it peaceably. Guests become less frequent; Matt and Rosalie Barker, Aunt Dell, the Hummocks and I see each other more regularly—they will be my companions during the long snow-months to follow.

In the kitchen and living room the fireplaces are lighted every evening. Sometimes they burn all through the day, while gusty rains strip the trees. This is the time of the stew pot, time to buy ground chicory to add to the simmering chunks of beef (a good t to the average stew along with a cup of fine ale or stout and *no* water, unless some is needed at gravy time). After the rains, come days of bright clarity when the hills seem to consume themselves on crimson pyres— weather for pot roasts. Time to haul wood, check the furnace and television antenna against October gales, time to start feeding the birds, to haul hoses inside. In the houses around our countryside the time has come for solid, filling, unembellished meals. At last the season is here for spareribs and rutabagas.

In my family it has long been the traditional dish to serve as soon as the days begin to shorten. At crossroads stands, among pumpkins and the last of the melons and basketfuls of winter onions and potatoes, the humble rutabaga waits. Often in the middle of the first comforter-covered night, while the shedding trees rustle outside, I'll waken to the remembered mellow taste of the juicy ribs and mashed rutabaga, as I think my father must have, and his half-bearded father and long-bearded father's father must have before him.

ᢒ᠍᠍᠍ SPARERIBS AND RUTABAGAS

I cook this exactly as my mother used to cook it. It tastes best on a rainy (or at least blustery) day when the fragrant steam will cloud the windows. Though the rutabaga is thought by many to be the lowliest of the root vegetables, it is one of the most heart-warming if given a chance. Years ago they grew strong and orange (though I loved them even then), but horticulturists today have bred them into delicate, pale-yellow-meated globes.

Peel a large rutabaga, cut it into 1" cubes, and let it soak in cold water. Salt and pepper 3 lbs. of spareribs, cut into serving-size pieces, brown in a little fat in a Dutch oven or large kettle, and when they are nicely colored, add water just to cover them. Add that trinity of spices—who first conceived this miraculous harmony of allspice, peppercorn and bay leaf? —indispensable to most of the stews and roasts that follow. Use about a dozen each of the whole allspice and peppercorns and a large bay leaf. Cook covered until the spareribs are nearly done. Add the rutabaga, a sliced onion and 2 large, peeled, sliced potatoes, and add more water if needed so that the vegetables will steam well. When all is thoroughly cooked put the ribs on a warm platter. Leave some of the meat juices with the vegetables, but if there is too much liquid drain some off and save as a delicious base for pea soup. Mash the vegetables in the remaining liquid until they are light and fluffy. Heap around the ribs. With this, serve rings of sweet red Spanish onion, well marinated in oil, vinegar, salt, freshly ground pepper and a pinch of sugar.

All autumn long, the season of stews and pot roasts continues. It is a good thing they require long cooking, for the attendant aromas and long low bubbling are part of the pleasure, while outside all is destruction and endings. These are the masculine months, the time of the warrior and hunter, the worker in the field with cold hands. After hours spent in the leaf-crackling, dying woods on cloudy or brightly illumined days (either for pleasure or labor, target practice, hunting a rabbit or felling an oak), one hungers for hearty meals. But too often such meals are likely to consist of thick, overdone slabs of stringy meat, with the vegetables garnishing them notable for quantity rather than flavor. While a well-seasoned and rightly prepared pot roast or stew and their gravies should be as subtly correct in flavor as a galantière of crayfish. No utility cuts of beef or mutton; but only the choice cuts of sleek steers, rambunctious lambs, or the milky meat of pigs still able to move about under their own weight (and with their odd, special dignity), should be used. No using a pressure cooker either—how can a gravy mature in fifteen minutes? And stews and pot roasts should not be cooked until disintegrated but until *just* done.

Nor need such foods be thought common fare. Near here is a theological seminary, where Father Quintana lives and teaches. His house is small, but from years spent abroad he has brought with him Renaissance tastes startling to encounter in a small Wisconsin village. The house, outside, is plain white farmhouse; inside, it bursts into papal splendor. There are crystal or bronze chandeliers, brocade draperies, Italian chests, Louis Quinze sofas, Persian rugs.

Father Quintana, at seventy, is lean and tall, but there his austerity ends. His home is never without guests. When dinner is served, they move to a highly polished mahogany table where ornate candelabra light up French china and old English crystal. The food is blessed devoutly—and blessèd it is, for amidst all this splendor waits a redolent, honest lamb and cabbage stew, a goulash or a sirloin pot roast with dumplings, or ham hocks and yellow peas. Despite his love of finery, Father Quintana was born on an Ohio farm and has never lost his taste for simple, and great, country foods.

These are wonderfully satisfying dishes, while autumn busies itself with wind and rain outside. They belong to the waning months, the time of the changing hills—as do, for instance, Aunt Dell's pork chop casseroles, the chops sometimes cooked in apple cider fresh from the mellow orchards, sometimes crusted with golden, home-canned corn from the summer's harvest. Or certain chicken dishes, prepared from the larger fowl available now. Now Ruth Hummock will kill her spring chickens, since they are hefty enough for one to feed her family and no picayune extravagance is involved.

"Why kill a chicken when it's still got a naked rump?" Ruth murmurs. "Can't people wait till at least they've got some meat on their bones?"

I can, if it means sitting down on a blowy October night to a Hen in Onions as Ruth prepares it.

✸ LAMB AND CABBAGE STEW

Brown in butter 3 lbs. of stewing lamb cut into small pieces and just barely cover with water. Add salt, a sliced onion, 1 t caraway seed and the trinity of whole allspice, peppercorns, and bay leaf. Simmer covered for several hours until the meat is nearly tender. Quarter a cabbage, soak it in cold water, and slice it coarsely. Add this to the stew, along with 3 or 4 large cubed potatoes and a few whole small onions, and continue cooking for another half-hour until all is done. Have a cruet of white vinegar on the table when you serve this and let the guests sprinkle a little over each serving. And use deep plates because the stew should be quite soupy. You mash the cubed potatoes in the golden gravy as you eat.

✸ TIP SIRLOIN POT ROAST

Use a 3 lb. roast cut from the tip of the sirloin. Salt and pepper it and brown on both sides in bacon fat or half fat and half butter, along with 2 sliced medium onions and 1 sliced carrot, letting these brown slightly also. Add a bay leaf and 12 each of whole allspice and peppercorns. A little parsley is good too. Cover and simmer until tender, adding water to make a good supply of gravy. When the meat is nearly done, add a carrot or two, cut into strips, and a bunch of scallions cut into 1½" pieces. Thicken the gravy with cornstarch or flour and serve with

✸ RAW POTATO DUMPLINGS

Grate 4 large raw potatoes into a colander that is resting in a basin. Let the potatoes drain well, pressing them with a spoon, and pour away the water into the basin, but reserve the starch that will settle in the bottom. Return the starch to the grated potatoes and add 2 beaten eggs, salt, 2 grated boiled potatoes and enough flour so that the dumplings will not disintegrate while they are cooking. Have a large kettle of boiling water ready and test one; don't add any more flour than is absolutely necessary or the flavor will be lost. Boil the dumplings, covered, about 15 minutes. They should be quite heavy and doughy. And be sure you make enough. There is nothing better for lunch the next day than the leftover dumplings, sliced and fried golden in pure butter along with any of the carrots that may remain.

੨ HAM HOCKS AND YELLOW PEAS

Soak 1 lb. yellow peas overnight, rinse, cover with cold water and simmer for an hour before adding 4 fresh pork hocks, 1 onion chopped, salt, pepper and a pinch of marjoran and ginger. Boil several hours until the peas and hocks are done, adding water as needed and stirring frequently. The last half hour add a small carrot grated and 1 medium potato cut into small pieces. Dish up the hocks cut into serving pieces and serve along with the thick purée of peas in a tureen.

੨ BEEF GOULASH WITH RED CABBAGE

Brown darkly several pounds of cubed beef stew meat in hot fat along with 2 sliced onions. Cover with water, and add salt and pepper, 1 t caraway seed and a bay leaf. Simmer slowly. About half an hour before tender, sprinkle over 3 T tarragon or wine vinegar or ½ cup dry red wine, and cover with a medium red cabbage cut into eighths. When the cabbage of this excellent dish is done, thicken the gravy with ginger snaps to taste.

ॐ HEN IN ONIONS

As Father Quintana is justly proud of the above stew, so is Ruth Hummock rightly proud of this one: Cut a plump but not tough hen into serving pieces. Dust each piece with salt, pepper and paprika. Add a little ground ginger too. Line a Dutch oven with many slices of onion (use at least 3 large onions) and lay the chicken pieces on this bed. Then cover the chicken with a handful of chopped parsley—be lavish with it. And for a final blanket use 3 more large chopped onions. Add 1 cup water and simmer tightly covered for several hours until the hen is done. Add no more water unless it is needed to prevent the onions from burning; they should not become brown at all but should be reduced to a lovely, golden pulp mingling with the rich hen juices and fats.

ॐ SMOTHERED CHICKEN

Here is another delicious, favorite method of preparing the larger fowl of this season. Cut a chicken into pieces (or use frozen breasts and thighs) and shake them in a paper bag with a mixture of pepper, salt and flour. Be sure the pieces are well coated. Brown them in a skillet in butter or chicken fat and arrange in a large casserole. Douse with paprika. Then pour over ¾ cup dry vermouth, ¾ cup cream, the juices from the frying pan, and enough milk almost to cover the chicken. Bake in a 375° oven uncovered, turning often and stirring up the sauce. The chicken should be very tender, almost leaving the bone, and the sauce thick and curdlike. It is delicious to serve over rice, either plain or fried in butter with a little onion and herbs.

ॐ AUNT DELL'S PORK CHOPS AND CORN

Brown 6 pork chops (for three hungry people) and put them in a casserole, salted and peppered, on a layer of thin-sliced carrots. Spread 3 T sour cream over the chops, brighten with 1 t paprika, and over all, pour a can of creamed corn. Cover the top with crushed cornflakes; over them, pour the drippings from the pan in which you browned the chops. The corn, cornflakes and chops blend together wonderfully. Bake this about 45 minutes in a moderate oven.

ᢓᢌ PORK CHOPS IN APPLE CIDER
For this dish, Aunt Dell salts, peppers and lightly flours the chops and browns them only until they are golden. For 8 chops, use 2 packages of frozen *baby limas* (if fresh limas are available, cook them first until half done). Put the chops in a baking dish; cover them with the lima beans and with 2 medium onions sliced into thin rings. Sprinkle with 1 t thyme or a generous pinch of sage. Pour over 1 cup fresh apple cider with which you have rinsed out the frying pan and bake 1 hour at 350°, adding more cider if needed.

ᢓᢌ STUFFED WHOLE CABBAGE
Sometimes, to match the plushy sunsets of autumn, more exotic flavors are desired. Then, any of the following three recipes is welcome. For this spectacular dish from a lowly cabbage, drop a large cabbage into boiling water just long enough so that the leaves will separate easily. Very cautiously dig out the core and spread the leaves apart, placing on each some of the following meat filling:

Mix together 1 lb. ground veal, ¼ lb. salt pork finely diced or sausage meat, ½ cup bread crumbs, 2 raw eggs, salt, pepper, a grated onion, plenty of minced parsley and a large pinch of thyme and marjoram. With continued caution replace each leaf as it is spread until the original shape of the cabbage has been restored. Tie it up well to retain its shape, cover it with several slices of bacon and bake 2½ hours in a medium oven, covered, basting it often with a mixture of chicken bouillon and white wine. Uncover and bake another ½ hour. The cabbage, by now quite unrecognizable, should be very brown, impressive and shapely on a large platter, and magnificent in aroma and taste.

৯ SPARERIBS AND WILD RICE

To serve six, use 2 sections of small, barbecue-size ribs, each about 15″ long, and brown them on one side. Make a stuffing by boiling 1 cup wild rice for 20 minutes, draining it, and adding 2 crumbled hard rolls, a finely diced onion and a stick of celery, ½ lb. raw diced mushrooms and ¼ lb. liver sausage. Season and mix well, moistening with butter and a little red wine, and stuff between the browned sides of the ribs. Sprinkle the outside with ginger; bake 1½ hours (covered) in a moderate oven, basting with red wine. Remove the cover at the last to brown the ribs.

৯ MATHILDE'S SAUERBRATEN

This recipe comes from another friend whose love of country, and old country cooking, equals mine. Marinate a 6 lb. round bone beef chuck roast in ⅓ part wine vinegar and ⅔ parts red wine for 6 days, keeping it in the refrigerator and turning it each day. On the day before the Sauerbraten is to be eaten, brown it well in beef fat or bacon fat. Add 2 large sliced onions, 2 T tomato paste, salt, pepper, 3 bay leaves, several nubbins of lemon peel, 2 good shakings of ground cloves, a few whole allspice, 2 t sugar, 2 cloves of garlic, and enough water almost to cover the meat. Simmer until it is tender, adding more water as it boils away. Remove the meat and strain the stock. On the following day, while the roast is

still cold, slice it diagonally across the grain. Skim 4 T fat
from the stock; in it, brown 4 T flour until it is chocolate-
colored, but beware of burning it. Then slowly add the remainder of the broth and let it thicken, always stirring. Taste
it; if it isn't tart enough, add some of the original pickling
liquid. Arrange the meat slices on an oven-proof platter, add
1½ cups red wine to the sauce and pour it over the meat.
Heat the meat through in a hot oven; just before serving,
brown the top under the broiler. You'll want dumplings
with this, of course, or

ཞ NOODLE PANCAKE

Boil 1 lb. best wide egg noodles in salted water, drain and
cool. Salt and pepper them well, add a little parsley, and fry
them slowly in lots of butter until a dark brown crust has
formed. Put a serving plate over the frying pan and flip out
the pancake.

ཞ COUNTRY ROAST BEEF AND YORKSHIRE PUDDING

But best of all, perhaps, while a hint of winter blusters
through the woods, is the aroma of a prime rib roast of beef
sizzling in the oven in a country kitchen. Buy only the choicest beef, with the bones left in, because these add to the
flavor and can be used the next day for soup stock (unless an
eager guest has gnawed away every last succulent shred of
meat). Score the fat on the top of the roast, salt and pepper
it well on all sides, and rub the 2 sides well with flour (and
at dinnertime reserve these end pieces for your two most favored guests). Now place in a shallow roasting pan, rib ends
down, and heap over the scored fat as much flour as it will
hold, patting it gently. This flour adds immeasurably to the

flavor of the crisp crust. Place in a hot oven, about 425°, modern theories of slow cooking notwithstanding, and baste it often and gently, so as not to dislodge the flour before it has mingled with the beef fat to form its splendid crust. For a 5 or 6 lb. roast cooked to pinky rareness, I rely on 15 minutes to heat the roast through, and 15 more minutes for each pound of meat. For larger roasts I use a thermometer.

For the indispensable Yorkshire Pudding, put 1½ cups flour, 1 t salt, and 3 whole eggs in a mixing bowl and stir in 1½ cups milk. Now beat it briskly until it is full of air bubbles. Too often this pudding is served flat and soggy when it should be crisp and puffed like a giant mushroom. The important trick is to pour the bubbly batter into a *very hot* pan in which at least ¼ cup of fat is sizzling; use the fat from the roast if you can spare it. Hurry the pan back into the oven about 40 minutes before the roast is done. For the gravy, thicken the beef drippings with flour, add water and a little Kitchen Bouquet to make it a rich brown. Serve the gravy over the pudding only; the delicate juices that will gather as you slice the roast very *thin* should be apportioned over the pieces of meat. Don't be afraid to cook a good-sized beef, for it is always delicious sliced cold. And for that piece still left over there are two more recipes, either of them splendid enough for a company supper:

৯ LEFTOVER RARE BEEF WITH SAUCE

Have the meat at room temperature, slice it thin and place on a warmed platter. Have ready a sauce made by browning ¼ lb. finely sliced mushrooms in 3 T butter, to which you have added ½ cup water, ¼ cup red wine, 1 bouillon cube, 1 t tomato paste, 1 t Kitchen Bouquet and a dash of Worcestershire. Thicken with cornstarch and pour over the meat.

Good accompaniments are creamed potatoes and a tomato
salad.

৯ LEFTOVER BEEF OR STEAK CROQUETTES

Put the cold beef or steak through a meat grinder along with
a small onion and a handful of parsley. Add salt and pepper
to taste, a pinch of cayenne, 1 T tomato purée or good chili
sauce and enough thick cream sauce to moisten it. Chill
briefly and shape into small sausages. Roll these first in a
beaten egg and then in bread crumbs; fry in butter until
crusty and brown. Serve the croquettes on a bed of spinach,
sprinkle them with chives; pour over all, either a tomato
sauce or a rich cream sauce to which an egg yolk and 1 T
lemon juice have been added.

One perfect day of Indian summer a knock sounded at
our kitchen door. Mrs. Becksmith did not wear a blanket nor
carry a papoose on her back and I suppose, for that matter,
she wasn't really an Indian though her hair was black and
stringy, her shape wiry and primeval, and her taciturnity
collosal. (Actually, she must have been German or Austrian
as was her cooking.) There was an angular loneliness about
her, and I swear she must have been summoned out of the
smoky mists brushing the hills, though a semi-truck as battered as herself stood behind her. Never did I find out where
she came from nor where, a few months later, she went.

I wonder whether, that first day, we communicated by
sign language because in memory now she seems hardly to
have spoken all the while she was here. She was uncommonly
grouchy. She let it be known that first meeting that she'd
heard I was looking for a housekeeper (I was), and since I
must be lonely up here on the hill (I wasn't), and she didn't

have any plans at the moment she'd be glad to help me out (whether I was glad or not was immaterial). Salary? Ten dollars a week. Working hours? She poked a warty fist against my chest and scowled like a tree toad. Working hours were not to be discussed, I was somehow given to understand with a belligerent grunt. I was to pay her the ten dollars and she would come when she wanted, right?

But then began wonderful weeks. If Mrs. Becksmith spoke little, she grew lyrical with a pencil stub in her hand. I'd find "gner pepprs" on the grocery list when she needed green peppers. Or "akla sitzlier"—she suffered from headaches. Or "oinoinions" or "ags" or "cron felks" (this last a poser, but Charlie down at the grocery store read it right off and reached for corn flakes). I was happy when she ordered "sparrowibs" to go with a rutabaga, and it took me almost no time at all to figure out what "toliet timsue" was. Nor did she hesitate to end her grocery list with sentiments such as "Im Godd we Trusk."

She called me Heth, or sometimes Hey Heth. She was spotlessly clean, and I'd often find her at such useful occupations as repairing the refrigerator, or my car engine, or building stone walls. She had a passion for stone walls and started half a dozen, finishing none; when she left, the meadow looked like a ruined Druid temple. Where she slept I never learned, though bedding was stored in the rear of her semi-truck. She loved the outdoors. Late one December morning I waited to hear her key scratching in the lock (she had insisted on her own key that first morning and I had not hesitated to give her one) but long as I waited, she did not appear. I never heard from her again. She was gone without so much as a scribbled "faerwall."

But she left behind her a wondrous collection of recipes

for dumplings, spaetzle, noodles, creplach—anything that would "go good" with stews or richly gravied roasts. And go good they did. The sight of a green fresh vegetable seemed to make her bilious; these she cooked in a rage, her antagonism seething until she could slap the harried and disintegrated spinach or broccoli onto a plate. But gravies and dumplings and noodles she loved. She prepared them worshipfully and beautifully.

I was lucky. Here are her best, as I learned them from her. I wish I had asked her to write them out.

ࢶ SPAETZLE

Mix together 3 cups flour, 2 eggs, 1 cup cold water and ¼ t nutmeg. Beat well with a fork; then put the batter into the icebox for at least 3 hours—this chilling is the secret of good spaetzle. When wanted, put on a platter, hold the platter slightly tipped over a pot of rapidly boiling salted water, and cut with a spoon into tiny pieces as the batter slips over the platter's edge. Boil covered until tender. These are perfect with any good brown gravy.

ࢶ SILESIAN LIVER DUMPLINGS

Boil some beef liver and grate it after it has cooled. To 1½ cups grated liver, add 1½ cups grated bread crumbs (and they must be from bread, not crackers), 2 slightly beaten eggs, 1 grated boiled potato, 2 T flour, a dash of nutmeg and salt to taste. If the mixture is not moist enough, add a little cream. Shape into balls and bury 4 small browned croutons in the middle of each. Cook in boiling salted water or stock 5 or 6 minutes. These are so delicate in flavor that I prefer not to drown them in gravy as Mrs. Becksmith did, but to serve them with browned butter or a light cheese sauce.

&❧ COTTAGE CHEESE DUMPLINGS

These, too, I prefer not to spoil with gravy; I serve them with a roast or vegetable dinner with melted butter or buttered browned crumbs and fried parsley. To a carton of creamed cottage cheese, add ¾ cup flour, 1 egg, salt, pepper, 2 T farina and 1 rounded t baking powder. Mix well, form into small dumplings, and store at least 3 hours in the refrigerator. To cook them, put only 1″ water in a large kettle, bring to a boil and reduce to a slow simmer, carefully put in the dumplings not too close together, cover, and simmer very gently until they have puffed up and risen in the water.

I miss Mrs. Becksmith. When a daily diet of dumplings grew oppressive and I pleaded for variety, she would substitute baked beans. The first time she baked them she asked for a bottle of beer. I cheerfully brought out two, plus two glasses. I was all ready to hoist my bottle to her health, but with a goddess-like scowl and a thrust of her chins (she didn't have double chins, just lots of them, all pointed), she slammed the glasses back into the cupboard. She looked at me as though she'd like to slam me there too, and poured her bottle of beer over the soaked, drained navy beans in their pot with onion, garlic, brown sugar and salt pork. That was how she baked them: no water, just beer. It is an exciting invention. Since then, I've substituted heavy ale and that's still better.

I'll always miss the cloudy face of Mrs. Becksmith around my kitchen. Each Indian summer I find myself watching the hazy golden hills, thinking she may appear again. But the mists just float away.

CHAPTER TWO

BAKING DAYS

Autumn continues over the woods and valley like a great, slow illumination. Strangely in these days of cessation, the light grows brighter. You can see far distances, and everywhere trees and hills are glinted with the red afterglow of summer. These are reposeful days. But in the village there is no such repose. One of these days a homemade sign will probably appear in the post office: BAKE SALE—PROCEEDS TO PTA—SAT. 10 A.M.

And SAT. 10 A.M. presents more hazards than one would think. The bake sale, held in the post office or rear of the grocery store or sometimes in the fire station, has aspects of slaughter about it. Every house in the village harbors children, hence every parent belongs to the P.T.A. and in each of these houses for the past few days there has been a chopping of nuts and rolling of dough and scraping of bowls, and the yeasty fragrance of homemade breads and rolls and kuchen.

This is the proper season for baking—wasps buzzing dizzily in last flecks of autumn sunlight, children rattling in leaf piles, the days slower in pace and growing nippy. Ovens that

158

have been grudgingly lighted only when necessary during the sweltering months now are lit with a pop of joy that relief has come. The comfortable baking days are here again and the women visit each other in their warm kitchens; the moment the baked goods are taken from the oven, they sit right down at their kitchen tables to sample them, hot and steaming, along with a cup of coffee.

On the morning of the sale the members of the P.T.A. have already congregated by eight o'clock, baskets and suit boxes heavy with their breads and cookies and biscuits. These are carefully spread on long tables overlaid with neat white paper, Mrs. Gardner's nut cake and Aunt Dell's rich rolls and Erna Mason's plum cake all displayed on paper doilies as grandly as in a Fifth Avenue confiserie window. All this behind locked doors, remember, the ladies carrying on like a meeting of the Gestapo. Then, once their wares are arranged, they swiftly start buying the cakes and breads from each other and sometimes even their own tortes; by the time the doors are unlocked at ten o'clock to admit the public (which I have come to conclude consists only of myself, childless, hence barred from the P.T.A.), there is nothing left to buy.

I reach out toward a pan of redolent golden muffins that seem still to be smoking only to have a small black cloth coin purse (of the kind my mother called her pocketbook) rapped sharply against my wrist. "Unh-unh," the lady smiles with unwonted fiendishness, "I've spoken for those. All bought and paid for. Sorry." I reach for a streusel coffeecake contributed by Mary Soderman only to have it whisked out of my fingertips into a black oilcloth shopping bag which I recognize as Mrs. Jeffke's. All the women look satisfied and there is a great deal of laughter. But man cannot live on laughter alone.

The air is tantalizing with the odors of yeast and flour and cleanliness and jams hidden inside doughnuts and warmth and the prickly sweetness of baked sugar and contented talk. Now, at four minutes past ten o'clock, the women are already closing up shop, busy exchanging favorite recipes as they leave.

At least I have salvaged some of these:

ॐ COUNTRY BREAD

I think the secret of this delicious bread is that it is baked in small pans. The half-sized loaves are crusty and, when eaten warm with melting butter, recall all that was good in one's childhood. Dissolve 1 package yeast in ½ cup lukewarm water to which 1 T sugar has been added. Scald 1 cup milk. Pour over 1 T salt and 2 T vegetable shortening in a large bowl and stir until the shortening melts. Add 1 cup cold water. Stir in the yeast. Gradually begin to add 5¾ cups sifted flour, stirring with a large spoon and sifting at the same time. Keep adding flour until the dough can be picked up from the bowl. Cover with a clean cloth and let rise in a warm place until double in bulk. Place on a breadboard with whatever flour is left from the 5¾ cups and knead until the dough is no longer sticky—the little air blisters should slap back at you. Shape into 4 small loaves and let rise again, covered. Bake these miraculous loaves in a 350° oven until golden brown.

Baking bread is a sadly neglected pleasure today. But persuaded by a taste of fresh honest bread even some of my most citybound friends have begun to take time out on a Saturday to bake a loaf. It's relaxing, and they hold up much better at the cocktail party later on.

❧ IRISH SODA BREAD
This is wonderful for afternoon coffee in front of a lighted fire. And easy to prepare. Sift together 2 cups flour, 1½ t baking powder, ½ t baking soda, ½ t salt and 3 T sugar. Cut in 3 T shortening. Add ½ cup raisins, a sprinkle of caraway seeds, a dash of coriander or cardamom, and a few nuts. Stir in 1 cup buttermilk, mix well, and knead on a floured board. Shape into a round loaf and bake at 350° for about an hour. Chopped dates are also good in this, but don't overload the dough.

❧ SOUR CREAM MUFFINS
Into a well-beaten egg, beat 2 T melted butter, 2 T sugar and 1 cup thick sour cream. Sift together 1¼ cups flour, 1 t baking powder, ½ t each of baking soda and salt, and stir into the cream. Pour into greased muffin tins and bake at 400° about ½ hour. Serve these piping hot.

❧ APPLE MUFFINS
This is a favorite breakfast muffin. Mix together 2 cups flour, 4 t baking powder, 1½ T sugar, 1 T brown sugar, ½ t salt and a pinch of cinnamon. Mix together a beaten egg, 2 T melted butter and 1 cup milk; stir this gently into the flour. Now fold in 1 cup of peeled, diced apples and a few nuts. Pour into greased muffin tins, sprinkle with sugar and cinnamon, and bake in a hot oven about 20 minutes.

❧ BUTTERMILK BISCUITS
Sift together 4 cups flour, 3 T baking powder, ½ t salt; with the fingers, work into this a generous ⅓ cup of half lard and half butter. Now add enough buttermilk to make a light dough (about 1¼ cups) and knead it on a floured board

only enough to make it smooth. Roll out ½" thick and cut into small biscuits. Bake them on a greased pan in a very hot oven for about 10 minutes. Split the biscuits and serve them dripping with butter at tea time.

૬→ BANANA PUDDING

Ruth Hummock bakes this pudding for the P.T.A. sales in an assortment of glass and earthenware baking dishes, gathering them back from her neighbors afterward. Grease a casserole generously with butter. In the bottom, place a layer of broken vanilla wafers. Then comes a layer of sliced bananas and a light sprinkle of brown sugar. Then a layer of custard. Repeat this three or four times, top with meringue and bake in a moderate oven until the meringue is tinged with gold.

૬→ PINWHEEL CAKE

This is the loveliest of the yeast-dough kuchens I know. Dissolve a yeastcake in 2 cups lukewarm milk along with 1 t salt and ¼ cup sugar. Add a beaten egg and 3 cups flour; beat, then add ½ cup melted butter and enough additional flour to make the dough easy to handle, about 2½ to 3 cups, though the dough should remain somewhat sticky. Knead it lightly on a floured board, then place in a greased bowl and let it rise double, which will take several hours. Poke down and let rise again until double. Now pinch the dough off into balls no larger than walnuts. Dip some of these into melted butter, then a mixture of brown sugar and chopped pecans. Dip the others in melted butter, then a mixture of finely chopped almonds, granulated sugar and cinnamon. Alternate these balls in a buttered ring mold, piling them 2 layers high, strewing a few candied cherries (halved) between

them. Let rise about an hour and bake at 375° for a little
more than half an hour or until done.

ᐫ❧ PEACH TORTE

Whoever bears this festive torte away from our village bake
sale is considered by all the winner. Mix together with the
hands ½ lb. butter, 2 T sugar, a pinch of salt and 2½ cups
flour. Press this rich dough into the bottom and sides of a
spring form and bake about ¾ hour in a 350° oven, watching that it does not burn. This shell should be baked the day
before it is wanted. On the following day, drain 1 qt. canned
peaches well, and place the fruit in the shell. Pour over them
a custard made of 3 egg yolks and 1 cup milk in which 1 T
cornstarch has been dissolved, boiled together until thick.
Beat the egg whites stiff, add 4 T sugar and dot the top of the
torte with this generously. Bake in a slow oven until light
brown.

"I'll bet you never got you none of my rich rolls and rich
sweet rolls," Aunt Dell trumpeted in justifiable anger after
one bake sale. I felt a pulse of hope at her outrage, for once
before I had tasted both her rich rolls and rich sweet rolls
(this is not merely descriptive but their actual names—"rich
rolls" and "rich sweet rolls." I knew they were incredibly light
and yeasty wonders, the best of all rolls). "You come by this
P.M., hear?" she continued hugely. "I'll bake you up another
batch."

I did—and learned one of Aunt Dell's secrets. When I
arrived, her enormous kitchen looked and smelled as every
kitchen should look and smell. Late jellies and jams, crab
apple and peach, were lined on the window sills; the cupboards and shelves were scrubbed to a polish; and gusts of the

baking rolls in the oven fought with other delicious gusts. What's more, rain had begun outside. It was an island.

She has two stoves: a very large and ancient, satiny-black wood stove and ("only for certain conveniences," she says) a gas range. She has made a great to-do about cooking everything in the wood stove—roasts, pies, rolls; she has been firm in her belief that decent cooking can't be accomplished in the modern ranges. She has always been evasive about giving oven temperatures when you ask for a recipe since, of course, wood stoves have no gauges. "Just good and hot," she'd say and look away.

But today, one of her sons, Buss, aged twelve, noisy and cheerful, gulping a Coke, came to join us in the kitchen. With horror, I saw him hoist himself up to loll on the searing top of the wood stove in which the rolls were baking. After a minute or two, he rose (still cheerful) and wandered away.

Aunt Dell burst into tears, not over her son's scorched body but because she had been laid bare: she had not used the wood stove in years. Rich rolls and rich sweet rolls were rising to their glory in the modern gas range. "It was Ma's, ainna?" she said, weeping, and motioned toward the wood stove. "I just can't bear to part with it; it's comfortable, see, like Ma's still around here herself. But if people knew I ain't getting use out of it, and just keep it around to make me *feel* good, they'd think I was crazy by the galore." She gave me a wounded-eagle look. "Ainna?" Big Aunt Dell wept silently and with dignity, all her warmth flowing from her as from a dozen wood stoves.

Then she remembered it was time to put up coffee and the thought and deed alone comforted her. The rain outside was a steady drenching. While the rolls baked we talked, stirring our spoons in her surprisingly delicate bone china cups.

Aunt Dell brooded momentarily, looked into the gas oven, but then broke into a smile. She had already placed two large glasses of icy milk and several pounds of butter on the table. She sniffed thoughtfully. "Sitting here waiting by a full oven gets a little *re*lax into you, don't it?"

Right as always.

ॐ RICH ROLLS

Both these and the rich sweet rolls are made from the same dough. Heat 1½ cups milk until it is warm to the finger; pour over 1 cup sugar in a large mixing bowl. When cool enough, add 2 cakes of compressed yeast. Stir 3 cups of flour into this, mix well, cover and let it rise about an hour until it is bubbly. Beat 4 eggs until they are light; add along with ½ t salt and 1 cup melted butter to the yeast mixture. Add 3 more cups flour, mix, cover and let it rise again for an hour or longer. The dough can now be stored in the refrigerator for several days if desired. Otherwise take a quarter of the dough at a time and roll it out, working in more flour if necessary. Cut with biscuit cutter, let rise until double and bake at 375° for 20 minutes to a half-hour in a greased pan.

ॐ RICH SWEET ROLLS

For these, roll out the dough, spread it well with soft butter, sprinkle with cinnamon, a liberal amount of brown sugar and broken pecans. Roll up like a jelly roll. Cut into 1" slices, place in a greased pan, let rise and bake as above.

Since the summer lake crowd is gone, Mrs. Brubaker ought to be gone too; but, unable to tear herself away, she lingers on each year until snow falls threateningly. Her gardens are covered; the sailboats have been docked in the huge, gingerbready boathouse; some of the upstairs rooms have been cleaned and closed for the winter—but still Mrs. Brubaker stays on. The autumn calm seems her own. She is there alone with her chef Eugene, one maid, and the chauffeur; and you'd think she would find it lonely, gazing out at the tall burning trees, remembering the crowds that moved and chattered under them all summer long. On the contrary, she likes it. This is the season when, she says, she restores order to her soul.

Eugene is a big help. Sitting before the fireplace in an October dusk that has come far too early, drinking coffee or tea and eating the remarkable seven-layer Castle Cake (and between each layer a different filling) that the cricket-noisy days prompt him to bake each year at this time—all this would restore order to the most turbulent and tired of souls.

ॐ SEVEN-LAYER CASTLE CAKE

For the dough, sift together 2 cups sifted flour, a pinch of salt and ¼ cup sugar. Into this, mix a whole egg and 3 T melted butter, knead until the dough is smooth and chill. Separately mix together 1 cup brown sugar with 1½ t cinnamon and several crushed stale macaroons. Divide the dough into 7 parts, roll out each part and place in a greased deep cake pan with the following fillings between each layer:

On the first, brush with melted butter and sprinkle over a quarter of the brown sugar mixture. On the second, place 4 T grated almonds mixed with 1 T white sugar. On the third, spread melted butter, a little of the brown sugar mixture and ¾ cup chopped raisins. Spread the fourth with currant jelly and strew over ½ cup finely chopped citron. On the fifth goes melted butter, ¼ cup brown sugar mixture and the juice and grated rind of 1 lemon. On the sixth goes another ¼ cup of the sugar mixture and a few chopped cherries. And to crown the cake, spread the seventh layer with butter and the remaining sugar. Bake in a moderate oven about 45 minutes. Serve plain or frost thinly with a hard, bitter chocolate icing.

Mrs. Brubaker's gentle fingers gracefully mound up the last cake crumbs from her plate and carry them to her mouth. Outside, the lake lashes in defiance of the ice sheet that soon will hold it immobile.

"I think I'd like to see Guatemala this winter. I wonder whether the air there would be satisfactory for Eugene's asthma," Mrs. Brubaker ponders.

I hate to think that soon she will be gone. In a flash I see the long, dreary snow-months ahead, without my summer lake friends, the young actors and the ingénue and the aging character woman, the Sunday crowds down at the country hotel, without Mrs. Brubaker and Eugene.

CHAPTER THREE

CHURCH SUPPER FARE

AUTUMN ALSO MEANS that we will soon be driving through the chill, translucent evenings to church suppers. There have been the walloping strawberries drowned in cream on buttered biscuits at the springtime socials on the church lawn, and also the sandwich- and salad-laden baskets of the church picnic in summer. And the fat, tender hot dogs dripping with sauerkraut and chopped beef sauce that the Christian Men's Club sells at the village ball games to raise money for a new altar. But none of these has the opulence of foods nor the special jocular warmth of the church supper.

Perhaps it is the coming into the warm, crowded, brightly lighted church basement out of the cold evening: here is friendliness and sharing, the basement redolent of boiling coffee, the women bustling in the kitchen, the children slamming slatted chairs, the men occupied at the tables, eating largely in silence but with rapt brown smiles. In part, too, it is the sense of revelry and release from the summer's hard work; this is a harvest festival, the tables heaped with prize vegetables and scarlet woodbine running like a river of fire among them—while over our heads are the sanctity and protection of the vacant church. And, of course, it is also the wealth of food, supplied by the women in a spirit of (usually) cheerful competition.

There will always be two ham loaves, prepared by two rivaling sisters-in-law, both tall and stringlike, both watching their loaves with hawks' eyes to see which is eaten sooner. One loaf is tart and somewhat exotically seasoned with curry and nutmeg, the other is studded with mushrooms and almonds. Both are richly pink, and each has a large boat of sauce beside it; but even on the sauces the sisters-in-law cannot agree. One pours the sauce over the ham loaf while it is baking, the other cooks hers separately. They stand like priestesses over their huge platters, on each of which are three or four miraculous loaves; Irene, once your plate has been heaped from her platter, will generously but dourly tell you that you must try some of Ethel's loaf too ("it's really quite good . . .") and Ethel, just as dourly but generously, will fill your plate from her platter until there's no room left for a peppercorn and then tell you to try just a sliver of Irene's ("it's lovely if you like funny spices"). Both platters, however, seem always to be emptied simultaneously, so the sisters-in-law remain good companions for another year—until a week or two before the next church supper, when their glances toward each other again grow apprehensive.

There'll be olives of all kinds, celery curls, carrot sticks, pickles and preserves and gherkins and corn relish, hot rolls and coleslaw, served warm as it should be. The children will be throwing coconut cupcakes at each other, until the pastor comes in, blinking and nodding all around cheerfully, not at all grave as he is on Sunday mornings after church in the vestibule. Our pastor, knowing the bent of the ham-loaf sisters-in-law, wisely if not charitably steers clear of the danger of having his plate heaped until there is room for nothing else, and heads first toward the casserole over which Mrs. Dolly presides—his favorite.

The casseroles are at one end of the serving table, under the old print of "The Angelus." Among them will be macaroni; what Mrs. Emlyn mysteriously calls her "chop suey"; and, in a rather small baking dish, Mrs. Dolly's potato pudding. The macaroni is rich with a sharp cheese from our local cheese factory and it has a crisp, bacon-studded crust (it has little relationship to the pallid dish often called by this name). On the other hand, diabolically calling itself by a misleading name, is Mrs. Emlyn's "chop suey." It is really a baked spaghetti with chopped meat, but refreshing in flavor because it contains almost no tomato. It is redolent of celery, onions, and the goodness of ground round steak—*not* hamburger, small Mrs. Emlyn will tell you with a warrior's thrust forward of her chin.

Once I asked her why so excellent a spaghetti should be called chop suey. She laughed with the merriment of a young girl. Behind her glasses (new-styled, with rhinestones) her eyes glittered. "Don't be silly," she said. "It's called chop suey because it *is* chop suey."

"But chop suey's made with bamboo shoots and rice and things like that."

"Maybe where *you* come from," Mrs. Emlyn answered loftily. For a moment, it even made sense. I don't know why. And I've never asked again.

It is worth its name, whatever it is called, and sometimes the pastor, out of a wish no doubt to seem impartial, will bypass Mrs. Dolly's potato dish and put a small dab of macaroni and another of chop suey on his plate first; but all the while, like Lot's wife, he is casting backward glances toward what to him must be bacchanalian anticipation of the potato pudding.

It is a simple, honest dish, easy to prepare. Like all honest foods, it satisfies more stomachs than only the pastor's. I've found since that it is a wonderful dish to serve with cold leftover meats; or for picnic suppers, instead of the omnipresent potato salad.

૨૭ POTATO PUDDING

For her pudding Mrs. Dolly grates coarsely 2 cups of raw potatoes, a cup of onions and a cup of carrots. These are mixed together, sprinkled with salt and pepper, moistened with 2 T cream; the whole is liberally larded and dotted with butter throughout. The pudding is baked covered in a moderate oven for 45 minutes to an hour, until the vegetables are done and a thin golden crust has formed. Uncover near the end if necessary.

The pastor helps himself to a self-indulgent, venial spoonful of the pudding, exchanging beams with Mrs. Dolly. Mrs. Dolly scrapes off some of the side crust which she has been hoarding for him with grim nods of her head toward others who may have wanted some. *Now* the pastor approaches the ham-loaf sisters-in-law.

"Why, Irene! Ethel! I didn't see you! I was beginning to worry we'd have to do without your wonderful ham concoctions this year!"

He laughs baldly, and the angels must shiver. For his plate is so crammed with the pudding, dabs of macaroni and chop suey, pickled peaches, dill pickles, split steaming sour cream biscuits oozing butter, that there is hardly room left for a sliver of each of the loaves, which the sisters offer him gingerly and in pale silence. I think it is not that he doesn't like the ham (he is said to have once been ardent toward it) but that Ethel and Irene are aging now, and that their battle began when he first came to the church (both girls were as yet unmarried). Whether the loaves were first offered as dowry to the then also unmarried pastor, I do not know; or whether the rivalry lingers, like so many, after its original motive has long since vanished. But the battle is still unabated, though the pastor has transferred his loyalties to another's pudding—that of Mrs. Dolly, who is his wife.

One leaves the church basement with a sigh. There are free movies or community singing going on now, accompanied by the peaceful clatter of the Ladies' Aid doing dishes in the steamy kitchen. On lucky years, as you step from the noisy basement into the quiet night, the year's first snowfall will have begun. All this lavish supper, plus cakes and pies for dessert, has cost a dollar and a half for grownups, half price for children, into which category husky youths of nineteen have been known to shrink themselves, especially if they have presented a ravenous mien to the kindly ladies who sell the tickets at the door.

&❧ THE BATTLE OF THE LOAVES

The recipes for the rival loaves vary in almost every instance where variation is possible. Irene and Ethel will agree on nothing—not on spices nor on method of baking nor on sauce. Only at the very root of the matter will the sisters-in-law concede to each other. Each begins with a mixture of equal parts of ground fresh ham and pork.

Irene's Ham Loaf consists of 1 lb. ham and 1 lb. pork, ground separately and then mixed together with 1 cup bread crumbs, 2 whole eggs, 1 cup sour cream, the juice of 1 lemon and the juice of 1 medium onion, a scant t each of curry powder, ginger and dry mustard, a dash of paprika and another of nutmeg. Bake in a roaster in a moderate oven for about an hour. It is basted with its own natural juices. Cover after ½ hour or when necessary. Separately, prepare this sauce: mix together ½ cup water, 1 cup cider vinegar, the juice of 1 lemon, a good cup of brown sugar and 1 T dry mustard. Simmer this in a saucepan for 10 minutes. Ten minutes before taking the loaf from the oven, pour the sauce over it to mix with the pan juices.

Ethel's Ham Loaf is also made of 1 lb. each of ground ham and pork. To it, is added ½ cup cracker crumbs, ½ cup sweet cream and 2 T dry mustard. This is pressed into a bread or loaf tin. Mix together ½ cup brown sugar, ½ cup wine vinegar, and ¼ cup water if the vinegar is too strong. Add ¼ t powdered cloves and pour half of this sauce over the meat. Bake in a 350° oven uncovered for 10 minutes; cover and bake an additional 45 minutes, basting with the remainder of the sauce. Then place whole mushroom caps over the loaf, stick slivered, blanched almonds all over and bake 15 minutes longer, uncovered. Pour off sauce into boat before slicing.

The macaroni and chop suey served at these church suppers are each hearty enough in themselves to provide a satisfying meal for any man, accompanied by nothing more than relishes and preserves and a good hot bread.

ᘓ CHURCH-STYLE MACARONI

Boil and drain one package of macaroni. Make a white sauce, about 2½ to 3 cups of it, and melt in it 1 chicken bouillon cube, stirring constantly. Then add 1 cup sharp aged Cheddar cheese, grated, a small minced onion, 1 t wet mustard,

1 t celery seed, and ¼ green pepper cut into small pieces. Fresh or canned mushrooms may also be added. Mix the sauce well with the macaroni, salt and pepper to taste, put in casserole and cover with strips of bacon. Bake about 1 hour in a 300° oven.

𝔝 MRS. EMLYN'S CHOP SUEY

Boil an 8 oz. package of spaghetti for 10 minutes, drain and (to the horror of any Italian people in your neighborhood) chop it gently into inch lengths. Add 1 can (1 lb. 13 oz.) whole tomatoes, salt, pepper, and 2 T butter and simmer for 15 minutes. Chop 4 large onions and 4 large stalks of celery; fry them in butter, or in butter and finely chopped suet. When they are half cooked, add 2 lbs. ground round steak (*not* hamburger, remember) and cook until done. It's the heavy dose of meat, onions and celery that count in this dish. Add the meat to the tomatoes and spaghetti, along with a pinch of cayenne and 1 cup grated Cheddar cheese, add further salt and pepper as needed, and bake in a moderate oven 20 minutes to a half-hour.

𝔝 WARM COLESLAW

Too often coleslaw is a soggy, chilled, unsavory mess. Properly and deliciously made, the dressing should be poured over the slaw while still hot and served at once. Have ready a finely shredded (not grated) young cabbage mixed with a little onion and, if you like, chopped green pepper. Stir together 4 egg yolks, ½ t dry mustard, 1 T sugar, 1 T flour, and 1 T melted butter. Blend with this 1 cup white vinegar and 1 cup sweet cream. Salt and pepper and cook over medium heat until it thickens, stirring constantly. Remove from heat and beat in ¼ cup olive or salad oil. Thin with lemon juice if it is too thick and pour over the cabbage immediately.

৯ CHOPPED BEEF SAUCE FOR HOT DOGS

These are the delicious hot dogs as served by the Men's Club at our village ball games; I have cut the recipe down to reasonable proportions, suitable for family picnics around the outdoor grill. Melt 3 T butter in a frying pan and cook in it a large chopped onion and 1 lb. hamburger until the meat is brown. Add 1 cup tomato juice or sauce and simmer, all the while crumbling the meat as fine as possible with a fork. Add salt, pepper, chili powder to taste, the juice of ½ lemon, a dash Worcestershire. Simmer about half an hour, adding more tomato juice if necessary to keep the sauce runny. Now you'll need an assembly line. One person chucks a hot dog into a hot bun, spreads it with mustard, and hands it on to the next person who dribbles over it a generous spoonful of the beef sauce. A third helper crams the bun with sauerkraut; a fourth, if there is room, squeezes in a strip of homemade dill pickle. These hot dogs cost a quarter at our ball games and nobody cares and the new altar for the church has already been ordered.

But before the great annual event of the church supper can take place, many meetings must be held. The color scheme for the decorations must be brooded upon. Decisions must be made to ask who to bring what; strategies mapped to prevent seven ladies from bringing seven identical Jell-o rings as they did one year, all having read the same recipe in the same magazine. The Ladies' Aid meets at each other's homes on the slightest excuse through late summer and early fall; naturally, these meetings would not be according to parlia-

mentary law unless they were accompanied by a lunch of mayonnaise salad, Parker House rolls, cake and coffee. Lunch is always sit-down in the dining room or at card tables on the sun
porch, and is served at four-thirty, so that those ladies who
must can hurry home, replenished, in time for chores.

Once or twice I have been summoned by a neighborly
phone call to sample what the ravenous Aid had left in its
wake. The hostess's husband and children still want their supper. A friend or two has stayed behind to help with dishes;
soon their husbands and children drop over to share the leftovers too. Astonishing quantities of food are always left simply
because out here if you're planning socially on ten, it is not
civil to prepare a lesser amount of food than would serve
twenty.

Husbands and children, despite their gruff scorn for ladies' fodder, seem to enjoy these hearty salads for their supper
as much as I do when I am invited to share the feast of remains (always served on the same white-clothed dining table
where the ladies first lunched, every crumb swept from the
white linen and the table set freshly and carefully as for the
first shift). I often suspect that the wives enjoy this second
party splash offered to their husbands more than they do the
lunch they have so thoughtfully laid before their fellow club
members. After all, it stretches out the party—the festive
mood hangs on. And putting one's best china, as well as food,
before one's husband must fill every wife's heart; these small
triumphs are part of what they've both spent a lifetime working for, aren't they? A wife likes her husband to see that she
can rise to these gracious moments. The men, though they
may eat mostly in silence, rise to what is expected of them
too.

"Well, Em," a husband will say, stretching away from the

table after double helpings of salad and cake, "did the girls like what you gave 'em?"

"I *think* so," Em will stammer, "except it seemed hardly no one ate anything. There's *still* a whole chocolate roll I'll have to put away in the freezer."

"All tasted okay to me," the husband says.

Em smiles. She has given a party, and won.

Two salads these hostesses are fond of serving each other are particularly good.

ಕಿ VEAL SALAD

Boil a 4 or 5 lb. piece of leg of veal, along with 2 stalks celery, 6 peppercorns and 6 whole allspice, in 4 cups water until it is tender. Strain the broth and save this for soup. Remove the meat from the bone and cut into ½ inch cubes when cool. Rub the yolks of 4 hard-boiled eggs to a paste. To the paste add 1 T butter, 1 t cider vinegar, 2 T dry mustard, 1 T sugar, 1 t pepper and salt to taste. Mix this well with the veal. Dice a third as much fresh crisp celery as there is veal and mix together. Chill. Shortly before serving dress the salad generously with special mayonnaise (see below), heap on a platter on lettuce leaves, and garnish with the egg whites cut in rings.

ಕಿ FRESH VEGETABLE SALAD

Into this go 2 cups cooked fresh or frozen green peas, 2 cups cooked fresh or frozen baby lima beans, ¼ cup pickled tiny onions cut in halves, ½ cup diced celery, ½ diced green pepper, 1 small can pimento cut into thin strips, 1 t celery seed, salt and freshly ground pepper to taste. Mix together and chill in a strainer to drain off any juices that might collect. At the last moment add 1 cup chopped head lettuce and

1 medium dill pickle cut into matchstick strips. Dress liberally with mayonnaise, top with a large blob of unsweetened whipped cream and dust with paprika. Sprinkle 1 t capers over the salad.

Once a heretic member tried to guide destiny by adding a cupful of boiled fresh shrimp to this salad; but the ladies agreed soberly that, though tasty, it was more like a seafood salad now and *not* vegetable salad. It is good though.

It is unthinkable that either of these salads, veal or vegetable, should be made with anything other than Edna Richardson's Mayonnaise. All of the women possess the recipe and any of them can make it perfectly, but Edna Richardson is always called upon to supply the dressing for these innumerable and pleasant meetings—it is like a royal prerogative. Somewhat surprisingly, too, since Edna likes to play cards for considerable sums of money, and many of the church women frown on this, particularly at her carefree habit of sometimes sitting in on an all-night game in which all the other participants are *men*. Yet all agree that no one can beat her at mayonnaise (just as very few, so the men have grievously learned, can beat her at seven-card stud).

Several times Edna has been out of town and so it has been the lot of one of the other Aid members to make the dressing. Then the women, sitting at table, taste warily, gently smacking their lips. "Edna does it different," they agree, though I'm sure this is nothing more than loyalty.

‌ EDNA RICHARDSON'S MAYONNAISE
Even when I have made this myself it has tasted irreverently exactly like Edna's. To 2 beaten egg yolks, add a mixture of 1 t dry mustard, ¼ t salt, 4 T sugar and 1 heaping T flour.

Beat well with a spoon or fork and add 2 T soft butter. To this add ½ cup white or cider vinegar and ½ cup water and boil until thick. Chill; when ready to use, add 1 cup heavy whipped cream measured after whipping.

ᙠ᠍᠍ CHEESE STRAWS

Though Parker House rolls are standard equipment at club meetings, some people may prefer these as lighter and more piquant to serve with an already rich salad. Blend 2 cups grated cheese, 2 cups sifted flour, 1 t salt, 1 heaping T butter and ⅛ t red pepper into a stiff dough with ice-cold sweet milk and water mixed. Roll ³⁄₁₆" thick. Cut into ¼" strips and bake at 425° for 10 minutes until golden brown.

Not unlike the church suppers in kindly ampleness are the funeral feasts of our countryside. Again it is the various sodalities and aid-societies of the village that take over. In the country, death is still an awesome thing, and providing abundantly for the bereft is a natural act to perform where the earth itself gives in such abundance.

Too, farm relatives come from hundreds of miles away to attend the funeral of even a second cousin, respectfully enjoying, at the same time, a reunion with relatives seen on few other occasions; and so death reweaves the cords of family unity. These relatives and friends must be fed after the funeral and before the long drive back home. Custom also says that the bereaved do not want to be left alone immediately; and so, from the cemetery, a stream of cars always turns back toward the home in which there is now one life less, to banquet and gossip softly around tables set up in a big farm kitchen or under the high trees in fair weather.

The mourners are well fed. "Clara will bring her *Kranz*,"

someone says, and Clara Dobratz always does—a delicate yeast dough pastry appropriately wreath-shaped. Neighbor women go to the house directly from the church services, so as to have everything in readiness when the grieving and hungry return. There is usually a ham in rye crust provided by the family or, in the instances when the family is unable to do so, by one of the church groups. It has been baking since early morning, attended by three or four women, and it is always prepared in the same way.

ॐ HAM IN RYE CRUST

A skinned, country-smoked ham, having previously been boiled, is sealed in a casing of homemade rye bread dough to preserve its last drop of juice and flavor, and to impart its own pungent flavor of the rye, and baked slowly until it is done. Then the crust is chipped away and fed to grateful, waiting dogs, the fat is scored and dusted with powdered cloves, spread with wet mustard and packed with brown sugar before it is shoved back into a hot oven for another quarter-hour or so to form a crusty glaze. The women carve it in the kitchen before it is served (somehow carving *at* the table seems too festive a rite for such an occasion as this); the sliced ham swims deliciously in its own delicate pink juices, all saved by the rye dough crust, as it is carried out under the softly bowing trees.

There will be creamed potatoes, of course, and preserves and homemade jellies, and if the feast is a large one there will be chicken to accompany the ham. This may be a Chicken Custard, pieces of chicken baked in eggs and cream over a layer of dressing; or buttermilk-fried chicken with biscuits baked right in the chicken gravy, the biscuit bottoms sopping with golden richness, green shreds of parsley clinging to their undersides. Plates are soberly filled with both ham and chicken, not too hoggishly this time, however, as the day calls for some special gesture of decency; the talk is lively among relatives who have not met for a while, there is gossip of Aunt Marge's liver trouble and of Cousin Mid's twins and of the color that Brother Joe is planning to paint his house, but it is never noisy talk. Even the children hang around their parents, a little afraid. Yet this is a *body* of friends. Even the widow, or widower, can manage the trace of a grateful smile, seated at the honored place at the head of the table.

Once ham was not served. It was Tom Ainsley's funeral and everyone knew Tom detested ham; he had sneered that it came from pigs. Ham might still have appeared at his feast had not things been taken in hand by Aunt Dell, who announced hugely and sonorously (and sincerely tearful, though she had never had much truck with Tom in life) that what a man could not abide as he trod the earth would not be served in his memory thereafter. Tom was a small man and a fastidious eater and had preferred greens to red meat. But he was also sometimes boisterous, surprisingly muscled, a heavy drinker, yet a good man who had fathered many children and treated his wife with the tender, careful love one might lavish on a small doll. His wife was twice his size, however, and all of their children grew to similar proportions; when drunk, he would call them a "Goddam brood of giants," his wife included. There was, however, his neighbors murmured, no sensible reason for his growing hatred of pigs. He simply called them big and dirty. While his hatred mounted, the children stuffed themselves with indiscriminate extravagance and grew taller and wider.

Aunt Dell (as big as his wife, which may have accounted

for his coolness toward *her*) loyally banished ham and decreed she herself would roast pork loins instead, seemingly oblivious that the roasts came from the same beasts that Tom had despised. Knowing the wonders of Aunt Dell's pork roasts, no one in the village set her straight; anyway, Tom's death, somehow, was not regarded as gravely as another's might have been. Secretly, the teetotalers in town remembered his sprees when, inordinately strong for his size, he had one time pushed over a neighbor's corn crib in angry pleasure, and another time had cornered each of his sons and shaved his head bald "as a sow's rear," he had said.

The feast, in fact, was nearly merry, though Tom's wife wept with the memory of his sober, solicitous, tender moments, and sometimes glanced with wry awakening knowledge down the table toward her fatherless children, all of whom were eating like pigs.

AUNT DELL'S BREADED PORK LOIN ROAST

This is delicious served hot; even more so sliced thin and served cold. Buy the best, most succulent, center-cut pork roast possible (having it boned and rolled will make slicing easier, though some prefer the crisp brown bones to chew on) and rub it all over with salt and pepper. Then sprinkle it well with powdered cloves and roll in dry bread crumbs (homemade bread if you have it; never cracker crumbs) that have been crushed very fine. The roast should be coated all over. Place in a pan with 1 or 2 bay leaves, 10 peppercorns, 10 allspice and a thin-sliced onion; place in a 375° oven for about 20 minutes until it begins to brown, then lower the heat to 300°. Baste often and cover the roast if necessary to prevent the crumbs or juices from burning, removing the cover again 15 minutes before the meat is done, so that the crust will be golden and crisp. If you like, add a few quartered carrots during the last half-hour, to improve the flavor of the gravy. Serve the roast sliced in ¼″ slices. This is pork as you have never tasted it. For the gravy, spear out the carrots to garnish the meat, strain the remainder and thicken with flour and water (but this is best eaten on mashed potatoes, not on the meat, or the pork's delicate flavor will be hidden).

৯ CHICKEN CUSTARD

Boil a 3 to 4 lb. chicken in not too much water. When done, remove the meat from the bones in large pieces. Reduce the broth to about 2 cups and season well. Make a sauce of 2 T chicken fat or butter, 2 T flour and the broth. Let cool, and stir in 2 well-beaten eggs. Make a dressing of the cooked ground giblets, crumbled corn bread cooked the day before and soaked in a little broth, a slice or two of dry white bread crumbled, 2 eggs, 2 T cooked rice, 1 chopped onion, 2 slices diced bacon, a large stalk chopped celery and a pinch of poultry seasoning. Salt and pepper. There should be 3 to 4 cups altogether.

Spread the dressing in a buttered baking dish. On this, place the pieces of chicken. Pour over all the custard sauce, sprinkle with cubes of buttered bread or crumbs and bake covered 45 minutes in a moderate oven.

৯ BUTTERMILK-FRIED CHICKEN AND BISCUITS

Cut a frying chicken into serving pieces, reserving the back, wings and giblets. Soak the chicken for half an hour in 1½ cups creamy buttermilk. Meanwhile make a rich broth from the back, wings, giblets and a stalk of celery. This will be used in making the biscuits.

To fry the chicken, remove the pieces from the buttermilk but do not dry them. Shake the pieces into a bag containing flour, salt, pepper and 1 T minced parsley. Then brown them in chicken fat or in hot oil and butter until golden. Pour the remaining buttermilk in a baking dish and add the browned chicken. Bake uncovered in a 250° oven until tender, about 1½ or 2 hours. The chicken should be deliciously crisp, and a good gravy for the biscuits may be made by adding milk to the drippings, thickening with flour if necessary.

For the biscuits, use any good baking powder dough. Reduce the broth until fully flavored (there should be at least a good cupful, however), thicken very lightly with cornstarch, add 1 T minced parsley and pour this into an oblong biscuit pan. Cut the biscuits ¾″ thick and place them next to each other right in the broth. Bake biscuits as usual.

CHAPTER FOUR

THE HUNTER

UNTIL a few Novembers ago I had never seen the eager inquisitiveness, the watchful impatience, of a setter or Irish terrier as the days grow sharp, the slate skies lower with their weight of snow, guns are brought out to be oiled and heavy boots to be relaced. The dogs sniff and circle and flop heavily to the floor only to leap up in a moment to sniff again, circle, flop. They pretend to sleep, whimpering through their fitful dreams of dry leaves and a far-off chuck-chucking of partridge —just as the men and boys, here in the country, thrash through their dreams of scudding rabbit, whirring pheasant, or ducks flying innocently low over a rush blind.

I myself do not like to hunt simply because I am disturbed by the pursuit, the panicky race for self-preservation and ultimate untimely death of any warm-blooded animal, large or small, vocal or mute. Once I argued the wantonness of hunting (especially by bad huntsmen who wound without being adroit enough to kill instantly) with a woman neighbor, an ardent Diana herself, if not so shapely. I told her of a rabbit I had twice saved one autumn from bloodthirsty dogs and how that rabbit became trustful of me, often sitting on the terrace of an evening simply looking peacefully inside toward the warm lights. And how, returning home one winter day from a trip East, I found that rabbit (I'm sure it was the same) lying on my back stoop, frozen stiff, dead. He had been inexpertly wounded by gunfire but not killed. His left rear haunch was clotted with blood. And, left to die uselessly in the woods, he had limped back to my house, thinking he might find rescue there again. I had been greatly moved by this petition for help. That, I told Diana, was a stirring trust such as brothers might have; it left me with little respect for the blustering, brawling killer. "Yeah," she answered with a vague shrug, dismissing any further silly arguments I might submit for greater kindness toward dumb animals, "rabbits dying on your doorstep. That's cute. But how often does it happen?" I suspect she missed my point and herewith return her bow and arrow.

For many of my friends are hunters and I do not hesitate to follow them through the woods. Though perhaps inwardly I am more often plugging for the hunted than the hunter, the exhilarating companionship and, I suppose, my own appetite conquer my dread of spilled blood. Illogically and even dishonorably, once the fact of death is accomplished, I feel no qualms at relishing the roasted victim. There is a paradoxical warmth and closeness in these slaughtering expeditions. Matt Barker, Hank from the corner garage and his boy, Chappie Wolf and Barnie Barnes (two converts from the city, snared for life now in remodeled Welsh pink brick farmhouses nearby) and their two young sons—these comprise the annual hunting party.

Hunting season usually opens with an all-night poker session in one of the neighborhood kitchens, the young boys allowed to sit up and watch until, like the dogs, they curl up dead to the world in spite of their anticipation. In the dark dawn before the hunters start through the gaudy or later on snow-crusted hills, Hank, a mechanic but nevertheless no mean cook, quits the game to fix breakfast. Nothing so ordinary as ham and eggs, but a thick, crusty, baked pancake speckled with bacon chunks:

ह HANK'S BAKED POTATO PANCAKES

Grate 2 large raw potatoes and stir in 3 whole eggs, ¾ cup flour, ½ t salt and 2 cups milk. Fry ¼ lb. salt pork in an iron skillet until brown and drain. Leave some of the fat in the pan, add the batter, scatter the fried salt pork over it and bake in a moderate oven until done. Serve the big, nourishing pancake with butter, syrup and jam. Applesauce is a good side dish.

These pancakes are a tradition of the season, as it is for Hank to cook the hunters' dinner at nightfall after the long day of hunting, while the men, wonderfully exhausted, red-faced and rumpled, sip highballs, yelling out to the kitchen, "For God's sake, how much longer, Hank, how long?"

But roasting the pheasant or rabbit is an honor Hank deserves. He is a slim, jumpy man and his face takes on the aspect of some woods creature as he sips and ladles. Wood smoke seems to wreathe around him as he bends over the oven in pious absorption, inhaling the mingled fumes of fowl and butter and spices. What he at last draws forth is, surely, worth the torment of waiting.

After the zestful day spent sniffing along fence rows or the edge of ponds, the dogs, already fed, sleep before the fire deader than the birds they have flushed. Barnie Barnes's boy, too young to hunt, along with several of his cohorts lured into the woods from the village by the magnet of gunfire, have molested the hunters all day by climbing nut trees, shaking the branches (and thereby warning the hunters' quarry away) to loosen the brown-skinned nuts. These are piled now in a kitchen corner, sacks of butternuts, black walnuts, hickory nuts. The half-starved kids crack them with hammers on an old flatiron and litter the floor with their shucks; if they don't eat all the nuts, there will be some left for pickling later on or to flavor cakes. The men have another round of drinks, each brooding peacefully over the carcasses of partridges or mallards hung outside in the frosty night out of the reach of prowling dogs.

But suddenly even the most tired hunter guffaws himself awake. Someone has mentioned Aunt Dell's husband. "You suppose Aunt Dell's got the goose done?" one of the hunters asks. For each year on the very moment hunting season opens, Ernie Dell, who is wiry and thin as his wife is otherwise, starts out abandonedly across field weighed down by his shotgun; and at the very same moment Aunt Dell providently shoves a goose into her oven. In all his days Ernie hasn't hit even a squirrel. He comes home at nightfall cursing and dejected but one taste of the juicy goose and he thinks he shot it himself. Aunt Dell does not disabuse his faith. He grows serenely happy and for weeks afterward we hear how he shot that goose honking overhead, how he took aim, one shot, right in the gizzard. . . .

Now everyone is wide awake, his hunger maddened by the fumes from the kitchen, and in a kind of desperation the talk grows heated. Oddly, all seem obsessed by a similar thought; in this comfortable, close-knit world of males there is only one subject left worthy of further discussion—how to cook a rabbit, a partridge, a pheasant, a duck, a goose, a snipe. "For God's sake, Hank, how much longer?"

ᏋᎦ RABBIT BAKED IN CREAM AND PAPRIKA

Either the wild or domestic frozen rabbit is good this way. Clean it well, cut it into serving pieces, and rub well with salt, pepper and a little nutmeg. Lard well with fresh butter and sprinkle on a pinch each of mace and either marjoram or rosemary. Add 3 or 4 fresh juniper berries if possible. Bake in a moderate oven about 1½ hours or until brown and tender, basting often. Fifteen minutes before it is done, pour over 1 cup sweet cream for each rabbit. When ready, thicken the gravy with flour and add 1 good t paprika for each cup of cream used. Serve spaetzle (see page 156) with this.

ᏋᎦ BRAISED PHEASANT

Quarter the pheasants or, if they are very young and tender, leave them whole. Rub with salt and pepper and quickly brown them golden in butter. Line the bottom of a baking dish with 3 or 4 slices of bacon and place on this a thin slice of veal steak which has been seasoned with salt, pepper and a little tarragon. On this, place the pheasant. Sprinkle over a little lemon juice, add an onion shaved into thin rings, a few peppercorns, and cover the birds with another thin slice of veal steak. Over the veal put 3 or 4 more slices of bacon. Cover the dish very tightly and roast until done in a moderate oven, an hour or longer depending on the size of the birds. The last half-hour add ½ cup white wine and a slivered small carrot. Thicken the gravy lightly with flour, add several T sour cream, and garnish the pheasants with lemon slices coated with chopped parsley.

ᏋᎦ STUFFED PHEASANT

For several medium-sized pheasants or a chicken-pheasant or a large roasting chicken or a capon (for any of which this unusual stuffing is equally delicious), soak ¾ cup wild rice in water for several hours. Drain and mix with ¼ lb. chopped mushrooms, 1 cup crushed potato chips, 1 small can water chestnuts cut into halves, 3 smoked oysters, 1 small minced onion and seasoning to taste, including ¼ t each of sage and orégano. Moisten with melted butter. Stuff the bird and roast as usual, basting with 1 cup imported ale.

❧ PARTRIDGE IN VINE LEAVES

Allow 1 small partridge per person. Rub each bird with lemon juice, salt, pepper and a light dusting of ground cloves and ginger. Wrap it well with bacon. Place in a shallow roasting pan and cover them with a layer of grape leaves. Bake until nearly done in a hot oven (this should be about 20 minutes) and remove the vine leaves and bacon. Turn up the oven very hot, baste with the juices and a little red wine, and let the birds brown. When serving, sprinkle the birds generously with browned, buttered bread crumbs. Decorate with fresh vine leaves. A few chopped fried mushrooms, the chopped precooked giblets, a spoonful of currant jelly and a little cream are good in the gravy.

❧ WILD DUCK AND PEA STEW

Halve the ducks and brown them in a good supply of butter and 3 or 4 slices diced bacon. Add 1 T flour to the fat, mix well, and stir in enough chicken or veal broth (or water if need be) almost to cover the ducks. Add lots of chopped parsley, a large handful of small peeled onions, a bay leaf, a pinch of sage, salt and peppercorns and a few whole cloves. Simmer covered for half an hour until quite tender. Add 1 or 2 packages of frozen peas, depending on the quantity of duck, and cook until done. Surround the duck with the peas on a warm deep platter, add a little brandy to the gravy and reduce over a high flame until nicely thickened and pour over the duck. A domestic duck cut into pieces may be substituted for the wild duck, but it will require longer cooking before adding the peas.

ࣾ VENISON HASH

Slice the leftover venison neatly and from the odds and ends make a broth by almost covering them with water, adding a small minced onion, a dash of Kitchen Bouquet and of Worcestershire, a lump of butter, a minced clove of garlic, any leftover gravy and a squeeze of lemon juice. Simmer for about an hour. Drain, season, and add a little currant jelly and some wet mustard to taste. Add the venison slices cut quite small and heat through only.

ࣾ HUNTER'S GAME SOUP

This is another of Hank's specialties, prepared when weekend hunting trips lead the men up to a northwoods' cabin. It is a rich, thick and wonderful soup. After the first day's bag he will select a pair of wild ducks or partridge or a medium-sized rabbit. Then the shack soon is redolent of them simmering in a large pot. The disjointed fowl or rabbit first is browned in butter along with a cupful of cubed lean ham, 2 chopped onions and a diced carrot and turnip each. A large beef soup bone with all the fat trimmed off is then added, along with seasonings and enough water to cover all. Simmer for several hours until the fowl or game is tender, remove it and keep it warm. Simmer the soup another hour or so, remove the soup bone, return the fowl to it and add a little chopped parsley and finely diced celery. Simmer until the celery is done, season further with a dash of Worcestershire,

1 T tomato paste and a little sherry or Madeira and serve with a bowl of fried croutons. Cooked wild rice (a few T) is also a good addition to the soup.

But a proper fowl or game dinner requires more than just bird or beast alone. Wild rice, red cabbage, ruby wine, certain tart jellies and fruits and nuts—all these are natural handmaidens.

ৡৈ WILD RICE CASSEROLE

Boil as much wild rice as is wanted until done. Fry 4 or 5 strips of bacon until crisp, drain and crumble. In a good bit of butter, cook several chopped onions, some diced celery and parsley until transparent but do not let it brown. Mix all together, including the butter from the pan, and add a good supply of sliced stuffed olives and some pieces of black olives. If the mixture is not moist enough, add a little broth or more melted butter. Top with browned buttered bread crumbs and heat through in a hot oven.

ৡৈ WILD RICE AND MUSHROOMS IN SOUR CREAM

This is especially good with duck or pheasant. Fry 1 lb. whole mushrooms in butter, add 1½ cups sour cream to the pan, salt, fresh pepper, a dash of mace and another of nutmeg, and a little red wine. Heat through, put on a large platter and surround with mounds of buttered and seasoned wild rice. Scatter crumbled crisp bacon over all.

ৡৈ RED CABBAGE

Melt 3 T poultry fat (goose or duck fat is ideal) or fresh bacon fat in a large kettle and in it fry 2 chopped onions for a few minutes. Add a head of red cabbage, sliced thin, and only enough water so that it will not burn. Simmer covered 20 minutes and add 2 chopped tart apples, salt, pepper, a bay leaf, 1 t caraway seed, ½ cup red wine vinegar, 3 or 4 T brown sugar to taste, and a few whole cloves. Simmer until done, about another 20 minutes, add a few T flour and boil uncovered another minute or so if necessary to reduce the liquid.

ᷚ SPICED CURRANTS IN WINE

Serve these as a royal embellishment to any game or fowl dinner, especially venison or wild goose. Boil 2 cups brown sugar with ¾ cup wine vinegar, ¾ cup port or claret, a stick of cinnamon, ½ t ground cloves, ½ t nutmeg, ¼ t ground allspice and ¼ t ginger to make a syrup. Add 2 cups of dry currants and a lemon shaved into very thin slices. Simmer until the fruit is soft and the syrup thick. Serve hot, or bottle and preserve.

ᷚ PICKLED WALNUTS OR BUTTERNUTS

Shell the nuts; if you don't have a nut tree, use the whole shelled English walnuts from your grocery store. Make a syrup of ½ cup white sugar, 1½ cups brown sugar, 4 cups water, 1 cup vinegar, 2 T honey, ½ t each of cloves, ginger, allspice, mustard seeds and curry powder and the chopped rinds of a lemon and an orange. Boil until well thickened. Add 2 or 3 cups of whole nuts, simmer 5 minutes, remove from heat and add several jiggers of rum. Bottle while still hot. Serve with any dark-meated fowl or game.

ᷚ HICKORY NUT TORTE

To conclude a game or wild poultry dinner, there is no better dessert than this torte, the tang of the woods still lingering in each slice. Cream together ½ cup butter and 1 cup sugar, add the whites of 3 eggs whipped stiff and beat until light and smooth. Alternately add ½ cup milk and 1½ cups flour, stirring all the while. Then stir in ¾ cup hickory nuts, chopped but not too fine, 1 t cream of tartar and 1½ t baking soda dissolved in 1 t milk. Beat well, pour into a buttered and lightly floured loaf pan and bake in a moderate oven. Serve plain or frost sparingly with a coffee or caramel frosting and sprinkle heavily with more nuts, this time chopped fine.

One perfect evening a really bang-up snowstorm began just as we sat down to a partridge dinner. The hunters' wives had joined us to make it a celebration, Hank had worked with fervor, cocktails had been soothing, and dinner was being served family style on the long oak table before the kitchen fireplace. We listened only in comfort to the wind howling outside—and up here on the hill on stormy nights it blows a tempest. Let winter come, we all thought, let it come. The snow flew like hunted white birds against the windows.

The partridge was so juicy and crisp-skinned, the wild rice smoky and the Burgundy so clear and dry that none of us bothered to notice the drifts piling six feet high outside. None of the guests could leave that night; friends slept cheerfully on sofas and mattresses in front of the fire, and in the morning we shoveled and shoveled our way down the interminable hill.

But even that had its own reward. The icy air filled our panting lungs. Inside the warm house the girls kept coffee hot and were cooking soup and baking fresh rolls. They opened preserves (this was the moment for the first jars of relishes and jelly, stored away in summer against just such a day) and brought up apples from the basement for a cobbler. Luncheon became as festive as last night's dinner had been. Through the terrace windows we could see the meadow, turned overnight into a river of astounding white; we looked at it with the curious mixture of half-fearful awe and exhilaration that comes hand in hand with the first severe storm and beginning of winter.

PART FOUR

WINTER REWARD

CHAPTER ONE

THE WINTER SOUP POT

WINTER MEANS BLOCKED ROADS, the fear that the volunteer fire department can't reach you if needed, cars that won't start. Often after a storm the snowplow does not arrive for three or four days. Trees crack from the freezing cold in the dead of night. The lights from neighbors' farms seem twice as far away. The rare friends who come to visit have a lust for driving into the nearest snowdrift; you shovel your life away and then the friend, dug out, cheerfully waves that he'll see you in spring. On a winter walk Mrs. Brubaker's house looks so untenanted, even in ill repair now, as to make me think she will never return. These are days of isolation and boredom—until I remember the companionship of a soup pot.

From Ruth Hummock I first learned of the dignity of the soup pot; she and it are inseparable all winter long. A pot is always on active duty at the rear of her stove, and into it go many unlikely things. Since her family is large and are sturdy eaters of meat, there are always big bones left from roasts or boiled dinners. Into the pot. Scraps of meat, a leftover potato or turnip, a spoonful of stewed tomatoes. Into the pot. A cupful of leftover sauerkraut, potato water, a chicken or duck carcass divested of every shred of flesh, a bowl of unwanted gravy, a neglected prune, a chunk of celery half chewed by one of the children (Ruth *does* cut off the tooth marks)—all go into the ever-simmering pot to make a surprisingly flavorful and varied broth.

When suppertime comes, the broth is strained, yesterday's bones discarded, and whatever amount is needed is ladled into another kettle to become the evening's soup, noodle or dumpling or tomato or potato or vegetable (the latter of course being least popular, oppressively loaded, as it is, with vitamins). Or nothing more than a store-bought can of boiled onions is added, which makes a delicious soup (though I also add a good supply of parsley, washed, dried, then fried crisp in butter, and a jigger of sherry and slice of lemon). And into the waiting pot of remaining broth goes more water, a leftover veal bone from noon dinner, a chicken wing plus a few scrubbed yellow chicken feet, perhaps a carrot, sometimes a shin bone or piece of rump from the fall butchering to replenish this magic cauldron for tomorrow. There is always steam on Ruth's kitchen windows.

A Frenchman thinks as highly of his soup pot as he does of his wife or mistress and this is a custom Ruth has inherited from a maternal French-Canadian grandmother. Sometimes, Ruth grins, a Frenchman's soup pot is as old as his marriage. Whether or not one feels uneasy at the occasional antiquity of Ruth's soups, it is always pleasant to walk into her kitchen on a cloudy, bitter day. The warmth and fragrance are compelling. The omnipresent and innumerable children dip in for a ladleful whenever they are hungry. It is stabilizing always to have a kettle of soup on hand.

I have adopted this custom without letting my broth become as mellow as Ruth's. After three or four days of haphazardly tossing in whatever may catch my eye and then savoring the resulting unpredictable but always pleasing broth, the dregs are tossed out, the pot scrubbed, and a fresh soup begun—a thick, velvety chicken and onion soup or a filling lentil and ham soup or the remarkable dill pickle soup. But at least there is always a pot of soup around, purring like a household pet and obliging as an old friend. Let it rage outside; the soup only grows thicker and better.

Whatever may be in the pot, it is always a hearty winter soup, supper unto itself. For a Sunday night supper party, a loaf of hot, buttered, crusty bread and a salad are added; the big, steaming, ironstone tureen supplies all the rest.

ᑫ CHUCK AND CREAM OF TOMATO SOUP

After several hours of tobogganing or skiing down the icy hills, this is a wonderful soup to come home to. To 3 qts. water add a beef soup bone, a 1 lb. piece of lean beef chuck, 2 onions, a few celery tops, a bay leaf and a dozen each of whole peppercorns and allspice. Simmer 2 hours and remove the piece of chuck. Salt the broth and simmer it a few hours longer until it is rich and golden. Strain, return to fire, and add 1 qt. whole stewed tomatoes rubbed through a sieve to remove the seeds. Simmer half an hour more, return to it the piece of chuck cut into small chunks, and bring to a boil until the meat is heated through. Add 1 cup light cream and just heat again. Try to find the old-fashioned oyster crackers to serve with this.

ᑫ SAUERKRAUT SOUP

Make a rich broth of a meaty soup bone, a piece of celery root or several stalks, a clove of garlic, 2 onions, 2 whole cloves, a bay leaf and seasoning to taste, and water to cover.

Strain when done. Add to the broth 1½ cups drained sauerkraut, a chopped onion, a diced carrot and a large diced potato. Simmer half an hour. Add 1 t brown sugar, a few whole
mushrooms and the meat from the bone cut into thin strips.
Simmer half an hour longer. This unusual soup is even more
delicious on the second day.

❧ DILL PICKLE SOUP

The friend, Jennie Dohmeyer, who gave me this startling
recipe assured me that it would be much loved by all who
tasted it. She was not mistaken. The recipe came from a step-
uncle who was cook aboard a sailing vessel during the middle
of the last century. In his own handwriting on faded paper is
inscribed: "You cook a nice piece of beef, not too lean, in
water, add a sliced onion, some cubed raw potatoes, and dill
pickles which have been sliced, and if too salty, boiled separately and the salt water poured off. Then, when the slices
of pickle, meat and potatoes are easily pierced, you brown
flour in fat and add to soup and then you add vinegar and
sugar to taste. As nobody ever has heard about pickle soup
when you mention it in company people look horrified. But
hope you try it."

You won't be sorry.

❧ LOPSCUSH

This soup was invented and christened in a farmhouse near
here many decades ago, on a wintry noon when five children
found themselves very hungry. Upstairs, their mother was unexpectedly busy giving birth to her sixth child. But the children were not without imagination. In the woodshed hung a
frozen side of beef. While one of the boys lopped off slices of

the frozen meat, the girls sliced potatoes and heated milk. It was all tossed into a pot on the range. A new soup from the lopped-off beef was born, and the youngest of the children pronounced it scushy good.

In a heavy iron cooking kettle, brown 1 lb. good beef, sliced wafer-thin in small pieces, and a sliced onion or a bunch of scallions in 4 T butter. Add 1 qt. loosely packed, thin-sliced potatoes, cover, and simmer until the potatoes are tender but not mushy. Now add salt, pepper, chopped parsley, a little chopped green pepper, and 1 qt. rich milk, using a little cream if necessary. Cook a little longer until well blended; if the potatoes thicken too much, add more milk. Serve this hearty soup piping hot, with crusty homemade bread, to a man who has just spent several hours shoveling snow.

ಊ CHICKEN AND ONION SOUP

With a salad and hot French bread, this makes a perfect party soup. Cook a large fat chicken as you would for ordinary chicken soup. When the chicken is just about tender, strain, cool the broth and skim off the fat. In this fat, fry at least 4 or 5 thin-sliced onions. Don't let them burn but cook them slowly until they are mushy and transparent. Bone the chicken, leaving the meat in large pieces. Reduce the broth somewhat; this soup should be almost as thick as a stew. Add the chicken pieces and onions to the broth, season well, add a little chopped celery and some whole mushrooms and simmer only until these are tender. Thicken the soup lightly with cornstarch mixed with water; pour this elegant concoction into a large tureen over toasted pieces of French bread sprinkled with grated Parmesan cheese.

ৡ BLACK BEAN SOUP

This, too, makes a noble party dish for a Sunday night buffet around the fireplace. Soak 2 cups of black beans overnight. In the morning, drain them and put them on to boil with 3 qts. water, a ham bone (or ¼ lb. cubed salt pork), some celery leaves, a diced carrot, 2 large sliced onions, ¼ t thyme, ½ t summer savory and a dash each of mace, ground cloves and cayenne. Sometimes I also add a small piece of lean beef cut into cubes for a richer flavor if the ham bone is not a substantial one. Simmer several hours until the beans are absolutely tender. Take out the meat and bone, and rub the beans and vegetables through a sieve. Return this pulp to the broth, add salt to taste, bring to a boil and stir well, add lean slivers of ham cut from the bone and a few splashes of Madeira, port or sherry, as you like. Serve in a tureen; float on the soup some thin slices of lemon and blobs of unsweetened whipped cream, the whole sprinkled liberally with the grated yolks of several hard-boiled eggs. Perfect with this is a tart vinaigrette salad of cooked chilled green beans, onion rings and either sliced water chestnuts or almonds.

ৡ LENTIL SOUP WITH PRUNES

Soak 2 cups lentils overnight. Drain the next day and add to them either a ham bone or a good-sized brisket of beef, salt to taste, a chopped onion, a chopped carrot, 12 prunes, 2 T each of brown sugar and vinegar, a pinch of thyme and 3 qts. water. Simmer for several hours until thick and done, being careful not to let the soup burn. If necessary, thicken with a little flour. Slice a piece of ring Bologna, add to the soup, and simmer 10 more minutes. This soup will keep several days, growing better each hour.

❧ CORN CHOWDER

For a quick and good winter luncheon soup, brown ¼ lb. cubed salt pork or 4 or 5 strips diced bacon, and add a minced onion, ½ chopped green pepper and a little finely chopped celery and parsley to the fat. Cook 5 minutes. Add 1½ cups water and 2 bouillon cubes. Simmer 15 minutes, then add 2 cups creamed corn (in summer I used fresh corn shaved from the cob) and 2 cups rich milk. Simmer until well blended, add 1 or 2 egg yolks mixed with 1 T cream, freshly ground pepper and salt to taste. Garnish this delicate soup with chopped parsley, pimento or a few sliced stuffed olives.

❧ BEER SOUP

Beer soup was a favorite of my grandmother's. It is a sweetish German soup which she loved for supper, along with a little fried blood sausage. Over a hot fire, stirring constantly, bring to a boil 2 cups rich milk (use some cream if necessary), 1½ cups water, 1½ cups finest strong beer or ale, 2 T flour mixed with 1 T butter, a slice of stale crumbled dark rye bread, ⅓ cup dried currants and the same amount of sugar. Cook a few minutes, always stirring, and add ½ t salt, a beaten egg yolk and a dash of cinnamon before serving.

Sometimes, even in winter, a thin clear soup is wanted as a first course at dinner, though served in all their naked clarity such broths are often unexciting. The addition of a proper garnish, however, will make them excellent soups. These three garnishes are always successful, the strained broth first being clarified by dropping a beaten egg into the bubbling liquid, then straining it again.

ᘒ CHICKEN LIVER DUMPLINGS

Grind very fine ½ lb. chicken livers and mix with a beaten egg yolk, a slice of bread soaked in milk and squeezed dry, 2 T butter, 1 t each of chopped parsley and grated onion, ½ t salt, fresh pepper, 1 T flour and ¼ t each of ground nutmeg and ginger. Fold in a stiffly beaten egg white, chill, shape into very small balls and boil about 5 minutes in the broth, uncovered. A little parsley fried in butter is also good in the soup with these.

ᘒ VEAL OR CHICKEN FORCEMEAT BALLS

Grind about ½ cup of cooked chicken breast or tender cooked veal very fine. Add the yolks of two hard-boiled eggs, 1 T butter, a pinch each of sugar, salt, mace, cayenne and marjoram; moisten if necessary with a drop of cream and rub to a smooth paste. Use 1 or 2 additional raw egg yolks to bind the mixture, shape into balls no larger than hickory nuts, dip into egg and very fine bread crumbs and fry brown in butter. Float these in the soup, along with a few fresh celery leaves, just before serving.

ᘒ BEEF DUMPLINGS

For a more hearty dumpling, mix together ½ lb. ground raw round steak, ½ cup bread crumbs moistened with beef broth, ½ t salt, some grated onion and, if you like, a bit of minced clove of garlic, 1 t chopped chives, pepper, a pinch of nutmeg and allspice and a squeeze of lemon juice. Bind with 1 or 2 beaten egg yolks, shape into balls and boil about half an hour in the broth. These are delicious in beef broth and also in vegetable soup.

And so, through the long winter months of dormancy, a country dweller chops his wood, reads by the fire, waits for the first cardinal to return in a red streak against the blinding snow, listens to the record player, writes a letter to Mrs. Brubaker or others of the summer crowd, and tends his soup pot.

❀

CHAPTER TWO

COUNTRY HOLIDAYS

AND THE REWARDS are great for the country dweller when the winter holidays come. Thanksgiving means remembrance, of course, and the turkeys, stuffings, relishes and pies of one's own childhood are always better than any other. Out here there is the added pleasure of discussions with neighbors for weeks beforehand—which farmer will supply the best bird? There is the constant scanning of morning and evening skies as the special Thursday approaches: snow would be perfect, but not too much to make driving hazardous for week-end guests coming to visit.

In the country, too, are the weeds, slim dark stalks of mullein and tawny milkweed pods, bright berries of bittersweet and garlands of ground pine to gather to decorate the house. There is the gusty wind at night, while you polish silver in the warm kitchen. Nuts from the woods are heaped in a chopping bowl, as they always were at my grandmother's house. Groceries are stacked everywhere; half the enjoyment of them is the trip to shop for them at the village store. Jellies and chutneys wait on the cupboard shelf. It is all prodigality and memory and custom. The stuffing and plate-sized slabs of white meat, the gravy, the preserves and dessert will taste exactly as they did years ago in my mother's house.

Hers was the best way I know of roasting a turkey, though the method may come as a shock to modern cooks dedicated to slow cooking and birds ignominiously crammed with a packaged dressing, then wrapped in a tinfoil shroud. Ready-made dressing? A cook of my mother's day would have thought a stuffing unpalatable, and insulting to her family and guests as well, if she didn't spend a good hour or two mixing it up—and with bare hands. As for cooking in a tepid oven to save shrinkage, who cared about losing a few pounds of flesh from a thirty-pound bird, if a brisk fire meant added richness of flavor and skin as crisp as fine parchment?

I think as good as the turkey dinner itself, when I was a child, was the hustle of preparation all the day before and on Thanksgiving morning; and the sleepy, sated men around the table afterward, pretending to talk, while the last of the cranberry jelly shivered away to a crimson lake in the hand-painted bowl. Reluctantly, yet sighing pleasurably, the women rose from the ruined table. Celery tops, olive pits, droplets of gravy, a blob of cream from the pumpkin pie, lay scattered over the good linen cloth . . . "Why can't you kids learn to eat like—well, like people?"

But the dishes must be done. The women clustered around the steaming sink like aproned priestesses around an altar, a little weary now but gratified by the rites they so properly and earnestly had celebrated. The turkey with its veal stuffing was a fitting offering to their gods—that is, to their menfolk and growing children. In their own way, they had given full thanks.

ᔰ VEAL DRESSING FOR TURKEY

For this dressing for a turkey of twenty pounds or more, my mother used ground fresh veal, a pound of it, browned in butter. Then ½ bunch celery and leaves, 2 large onions, 2 winter apples and 3 or 4 medium carrots went through the food grinder; this aromatic mixture, along with the veal and its juices, was added to as much crumbled stale bread as was needed. It was homemade bread, too, and sometimes a cup of leftover johnnycake or corn meal muffins was thrown in, all previously soaked in rich milk and squeezed as dry as two plump, strong hands could squeeze it. Then plenty of salt and pepper, sage or poultry seasoning to taste, and an egg or two if the stuffing needed binding. It was a moist dressing, and the best I know.

And the turkey was filled and trussed the evening before, to lie overnight in the chilly back hall where the cranberries already were jelling in the shiny, priceless, hand-painted bowl that had been a wedding gift to my parents. Some children prefer the expectancy of the night before Christmas. I preferred (and still do) this evening, and sneaking out to the back hall to stand in reverence before the great stout bird.

And the next morning—how were the women going to get everything done before the company came? Uncles and aunts soon arrived, my mother shrieking at them to wipe their shoes clean in the front hall. My sister had finished setting the gleaming table. Aunt Ida would wipe an imaginary speck of dust from the turkey platter, while Aunt Elsa reminded my mother to save the heart and a piece of liver for her. Uncle Albert and my father would grumble because dinner was late— it was nearly one o'clock. . . .

The waiting was agonizing; it still is today, for we stuff and roast our turkey precisely, and with as delectable results, as my mother did.

&❧ THE PROPER WAY TO ROAST A LARGE TURKEY

The ritual of roasting the turkey began when my mother steamed the turkey, and this perhaps will shock today's cooks. But it is also the secret of keeping the meat moist and flavorsome. In the enormous, tightly covered roaster, it bathed in a quart of steaming water for half an hour over a moderate flame. Then the water was drained off, and the turkey was dried as neatly as a baby (with snowy dish towels still fragrant with the icy wind in which they had flapped dry on wash day). Then it was rubbed with salt, then lavishly spread with butter, at least ½ lb. of it. The water in which it had steamed was carefully hoarded to be used later for basting. And the turkey, seeming to groan with satisfaction, then was shoved into a *hot* oven and basted often with the melted butter. Only later, when it began to brown as richly as autumn leaves, was the heat lowered. Now endless basting began with the water saved from the steaming. Incredible aromas filled the kitchen. A turkey previously steamed does not take so long to roast, remember; and if it becomes too brown, it should be covered, but the cover should be removed again near the end to allow the skin to become crisp.

At last came the moment almost too suspenseful to bear, for it meant that soon the crisp, hallowed bird would be borne to table. It came when my mother poured a half-pint bottle of light cream over the turkey—say, 15 minutes before it was done. Later, flour thickening and the remaining steam-

ing-water were added to the gravy, which bubbled to a
golden deliciousness.

A cold turkey sandwich with homemade mayonnaise and
a glass of icy milk before bedtime are always part of the holiday ritual we observe, as is turkey hash for lunch the next day,
the remnants of dressing, gravy and turkey snibbles heated together with a spurt of sherry, and served with a casserole of
noodles in sour cream. But with luck and foresight, generous
portions of meat still cling to the breastbone and second
joints. These pieces are trimmed carefully from the carcass
(which itself is saved for soup, thus making the turkey an economical bird indeed); usually for the Saturday or Sunday night
supper after Thanksgiving, they become the mainstay of a
bubbly concoction rich in wine and cream and cheese, and a
satisfying relief from the customary hash and more hash. Even
turkey can become boring, though I'd not admit it on the days
before Thanksgiving. This dish will rekindle interest and appetite on the days after.

&ᴥ TURKEY LEFTOVERS IN WHITE WINE SAUCE
Cut the leftover turkey, preferably the breast, into neat, thin
slices. Lay these generously over pieces of good crisp toast in
a flat baking dish or individual casseroles. Sprinkle over some
halved mushrooms, previously browned in butter. Now pour
over a good amount of cream sauce, seasoned with a little
rosemary, and to which you have added dry white wine or
sherry to taste. Shake enough grated Parmesan cheese over
the top to make a nice coating, add a few slivered almonds if
you like and some chopped parsley, dot well with butter and
put in a hot oven for a few minutes, just long enough to heat

the dish through. Then run under the broiler until the cheese and sauce form a bubbly, golden crust.

୫ NOODLES IN SOUR CREAM
Boil and drain a package of wide noodles. Dress lightly with butter, salt and pepper, stir in ½ cup unsweetened whipped cream, ½ cup sour cream, 2 egg yolks, ½ cup buttered and browned crumbs, and bake in a buttered casserole in a moderate oven for about half an hour.

Possibly your preference is for a fowl other than turkey on Thanksgiving Day. As the veal stuffing seems to me indispensable to a turkey, there are two stuffings created especially to grace the insides of a duck or goose.

୫ SAUERKRAUT STUFFING FOR DUCK
Drain and chop coarsely 2 cups of sauerkraut. Season with salt, pepper, a pinch of thyme, 1 T brown sugar, 1 chopped clove garlic, and add a large chopped onion, a tart apple (peeled, cored and chopped) and ¾ cup diced and partly fried salt pork. A few raisins or currants and chopped water chestnuts are good too. Moisten with a jigger of brandy, stuff the duck lightly and baste the bird with red wine while roasting as usual.

୫ COUNTRY STUFFING FOR GOOSE
The fruits of the trees, the nuts on the bough, the grunting pig in the barnyard—all become part of this delicious dressing. Roast and peel 1 lb. chestnuts and chop them. Fry brown ½ lb. sausage meat. Mix together with 2 peeled and chopped fresh pears, 10 chopped prunes previously soaked in water, salt, pepper, ½ t marjoram or rosemary, a small chopped onion, a stick of celery minced and several cups of

dry bread crumbs. Moisten with a little sherry and enough melted butter to hold the stuffing together.

Then comes Christmas.

From Mrs. Brubaker wintering out in Arizona, there has already arrived the hoped-for gift of six precious jars of Eugene's stuffed, rum-soaked prunes, of which he brags all summer long, and well he might. A few relatives and friends arrive to spend the holidays and to help decorate the tree, not inside the house but out on the front terrace, hung with yards of tinsel and glittering ornaments, gold and silver, cut from tin cans saved all year. Seen through the living room windows at night, lit with green and amber light, it is stately and silent, the meadow black beyond it. It seems part of earth, not manmade.

The Stollen from Aunt Elsa is late in arriving—worrisomely, for homemade nut- and cherry-strewn Stollen for breakfast on Christmas morning has long been a tradition in my family. But one day the package is waiting in the post office in the village, along with a gift from the postmistress—a box of her homemade sugar plums (which I had thought were only the fantasy of some ancient storyteller's imagination, until I tasted one; hers is an old New England recipe). The Stollen, sugar plums, stuffed prunes are true Christmas presents, as is that of Father Quintana. After midnight Mass he ploughs through the snow in his station wagon like a speed-happy Magus, arriving with a generous gift of his own spicy, heady chutney. There is a late buffet waiting for him. Ham baked in a rye crust—baked for no special meal, but only to have on hand for guests at any time of night or day through the holidays; it is served sliced cold in thin curls on a big platter, drenched with a pomegranate sauce kept ready all Christmas week in the icebox. Beside it, since he likes sweets even at three o'clock in the morning after a good number of highballs (as do some of the less bibulous ladies) waits a punch bowl filled with a light and lovely old-fashioned dessert: blobs of meringue drifting on a lake of custard and called, as long as I can remember, Floating Island.

On Christmas morning the buttered Stollen is eaten while dozens of cups of coffee are consumed. The meadow is white and vast; the hills white and rolling. The Christmas dinner (turkey again) is in the oven. Some house guests are skiing; others, though thinking themselves less venturesome, are making far more perilous descents down the rocky hills in a coasting pan. But before dinner I pay calls on neighbors if I can sneak out between other neighbors paying calls on me. At the Barkers' I am handed a plate of almond-and-wine cakes, which Rosalie passes around accompanied by a chaste, gentle glass of her homemade dandelion wine (which has also gone into the cookies). Matt turns his drink down and glumly announces that they were just planning to call on me—at my house he gets Martinis.

At Ruth Hummock's across the road, I find a loud, cheerful, women's house because all her men, from the fourteen-year-old on up, have been down at the corner tavern since noon dinner. And here I collect more bounty—a half-gallon jar of homemade sauerkraut and a dressed, frozen rooster which, she says with a husky but modest chuckle, she "had made into a capon especially." And still another gift: a friend of Ruth's, prosperous enough to winter in Florida, has sent them a crate of succulent, tree-ripened oranges. But Ruth's canned-juice-bred children won't eat them, saying they taste funny. And so, the case of marvelous and rare, really ripe and undyed fruit is loaded into my car. Ruth is relieved to have the odd things out of her kitchen shed.

Back home, some of my ex-city neighbors have dropped in. They look ruddy and bright. Helen has bought her husband, Mac, a new oil burner for Christmas for the old farmhouse they're remodeling. Mac, turned week-end painter since leaving town, has given Helen a gouache self-portrait which (to me at least) is somewhat mystifying, since it shows him sitting in a model T bathtub with autumn leaves falling on his hair. But both look satisfied and feel the gifts are a fair exchange. We drink Martinis on it. Like a summoned genie, a face appears at the kitchen door: Matt Barker. As we insist he have a Martini, his face lights like an eastern star. But Rosalie is waiting in the car. We urge her in, blushing and protesting. Now after a few rounds of drinks, the turkey is ready to come out of the oven, so everyone may as well stay on and more plates are added to the long table. . . .

This is Christmas in the country today.

ළ⊷ CHRISTMAS STOLLEN

Make a sponge by mixing together 2 cups warm milk, a little sugar, 1 cup flour and 2 yeastcakes dissolved in a small amount of warm milk. Set it aside to rise. Now in your largest mixing bowl combine ½ lb. melted butter, ½ lb. melted lard or vegetable shortening, 1 T goose fat if possible, 6 beaten eggs, 2 cups sugar, 2 cups warm milk, 1 rounded t salt, 1 t grated nutmeg, 1 grated lemon rind, 1 cup raisins, and ¾ lb. mixed candied fruits and ¼ lb. blanched almonds which have been run together coarsely through the food chopper. Add to all this the sponge and enough additional flour (about 12 cups) to make a stiff dough. Knead it well. Cover and let it rise overnight. In the morning, shape into 6 long loaves, buttering the tops and lopping them over. Let rise again and bake at 350° for 30 or 40 minutes. Frost while still warm with an icing of powdered sugar and cream; decorate the tops with blanched slivered almonds, citron and candied cherries. Wrapped in snowy dish towels, these will keep all through the holidays.

৯ SUGAR PLUMS

Grind up some dried fruits—apricots, peaches, figs, pears, apples, prunes—along with some walnuts or filberts and some lemon peel, fresh or candied. Moisten part of the mixture with dark rum and the remainder with fine brandy, enough to bind all the ingredients together. Shape into small plums and roll in granulated sugar several times, repeating as the plums absorb the sugar. They will keep best in the refrigerator and mellow with time. Don't give this confection to young children no matter what they've read in fairy tales.

৯ STUFFED PRUNES

Use these to garnish the Christmas fowl or serve them with roast pork or veal. Make a syrup of 4 cups brown sugar, 1 cup good vinegar, 5 cups water, several broken sticks of cinnamon, a dozen whole cloves, ¼ t ground allspice, 2 T honey; add to it 1 lb. largest dried prunes, half an orange with rind cut into thin slices, and the same of lemon. Boil for an hour. Strain the prunes from the syrup, remove the pits carefully and stuff each prune with a walnut, or some with whole blanched almonds. Place the prunes in jars, inserting the orange and lemon slices among them along with some pieces of candied ginger, and place the jars in a pan of water. Bring the water to a boil and when the prunes are again heated through, pour over them 2 jiggers of best rum and fill the jars with boiling syrup.

৵ CHUTNEY

Father Quintana's chutney can be made quickly and easily and is a perfect condiment for cold leftover fowl. Chop a can of pineapple (No. 2½) into fine pieces, reserving all the juices. Also chop very fine ½ lb. blanched almonds and a walnut-sized piece of fresh ginger. Combine these with the pineapple juice, 2 cups brown sugar, a clove of garlic, ½ cup wine vinegar and 1 cup cider vinegar, ½ lb. raisins, ½ lb. currants, ¾ t salt, ¼ t pepper; boil for 20 minutes. Fish out the clove of garlic if possible and seal the chutney in sterilized jars with paraffin.

৵ ALMOND WINE CAKES

Cream ¼ lb. butter and gradually work in ⅓ cup sugar and 2 egg yolks and beat until fluffy. Now stir in ½ cup almonds, ground not too fine, a little grated lemon rind and ¼ t anise extract. Add 4 T dandelion wine (I use any of the sweet white wines or sherry), 1 cup flour and a pinch of salt. Spread more chopped almonds on a sheet of wax paper, drop the batter on them by tablespoonfuls, and coat the cakes well with the nuts. Bake at 400° for about 15 minutes or until pale gold.

৵ HAM WITH POMEGRANATE SAUCE

Slice baked ham into thin curls or cut it into julienne strips. Combine with half the amount of Swiss cheese cut into julienne. For the dressing, beat together with a fork ¾ cup salad or olive oil, ⅛ cup wine vinegar, ⅛ cup lemon juice, ½ t wet mustard, 1 scant t sugar, 1 t sour cream, and salt and pepper to taste. Add the ruby seeds scooped out of a pomegranate and marinate several hours. To serve, heap the ham and cheese on a bed of romaine or Bibb lettuce or watercress and pour over the dressing. There are various good garnishes. A molded wine-flavored fresh fruit gelatin salad is excellent, or brandied peaches or stuffed prunes may be used, or quartered hard-boiled eggs and fat black olives. Buttered pumpernickel always accompanies this; it is a relief from the ham-on-buns and turkey-on-buns one is apt to meet at every holiday open house.

ε⊷ OLD-FASHIONED FLOATING ISLAND

This pleasant light dessert has nearly vanished from today's dinner tables, yet it is wonderfully satisfying after a heavy meal. Put 1 qt. milk to boil in a double boiler. Beat the whites of 4 eggs until stiff, and drop them a spoonful at a time on top of the boiling milk. Cook 1 minute and remove with a skimmer. Now beat together the 4 egg yolks, ½ cup sugar and 1 T cornstarch. When light, add to the milk and cook, constantly stirring, until thick. Remove from fire, add 1 t vanilla, let cool and pour into a large fancy bowl or sherbet glasses. Heap the egg whites on top, dot with currant jelly and chill. Sometimes I omit the currant jelly and, just before serving, pour over a little raspberry or cherry cordial or kirsch.

ε⊷ AMBROSIA

This is a staple dessert of Aunt Dell's festive tables and now often of ours. Combine equal parts of fresh grated coconut (let the men of the house crack the coconut and the kids drink the milk—it's part of the holiday fun) and the cubed pulp of fresh oranges. Add a few raisins and broken pecans; sprinkle very sparingly with sugar to taste. To be refrigerated overnight in a cut glass bowl, Aunt Dell says.

🌳

CHAPTER THREE

THE BLIZZARD CUPBOARD

THE NIGHT OF the partridge dinner and the unexpected, un-
heeded snowstorm that locked us all in overnight taught me
the wisdom of a Blizzard Cupboard. We may at any time during the winter be stranded for half a week, comfortably, enjoyably, but also hungrily since we do not use a deep freeze
(the meats and vegetables of the countryside in summer and
of the markets in neighboring towns in winter being too
bountiful). Helpful as frozen foods may be, or economical,
the fresh is always better.

A blizzard in the country has great beauty but also terror.
The trees whip, the sky vanishes, the snow moves on you like
a white army while the wind sings demoniac hymns. Watched
safely from the wall of windows facing the meadow, your back
to the fireplace, there are few more spectacular sights. When
the storm is over you waken in an unknown world. The hills
have moved; the meadow seems to tip; where there were hollows there are wavelike crests; shrubs and small trees have vanished under drifts; the picnic table has become a sarcophagus
of snow. A gust of wind ripples the brittle sunlit treetops and
they burst into blue and magenta, green and golden flame.

It is exhilarating and you long to explore this new land—but step outside and all the glory is gone. Doorways are blocked and you force an opening only to find the road has vanished. The plows are already out but main highways and county trunk roads must be cleared first. It is sometimes four or five days before the private roads are reached. And a quarter-mile-long driveway of six-foot drifts is more than a dozen men with shovels could face with spirit. It is a breathless enough task to explore one's way to the woodpile. Nor can the mailbox be reached. Gods and monarchs may travel through such crystal beauty, but not you.

There is little else to do but return inside and telephone neighbors (if the lines are not down) to hear what calamities they may have suffered and to report on one's own welfare. For this isolation is, its hazards notwithstanding, a time of warm, neighborly excitement. Weather in the country is always a major and binding event. All reports in, there is little left to do but light the fireplaces, haul out books and magazines, tune in the excellent symphonic broadcasts of our state FM station, and dream of how to ransack the Blizzard Cupboard most enticingly at the end of the lonely if lovely day. . . .

On such days, though it is small, the cupboard becomes a great warehouse. Actually it is no more than a modest but well-chosen cache of canned and bottled goods, kept separate from other supplies and intended for use only in an emergency. On its shelves are the good newer soups, canned luncheon meats and hash and corned beef, Chinese vegetables and fried noodles, canned milk, mushrooms, tomato sauce, a package of lentils, another of almonds, bouillon cubes, boned chicken, lobster, brown bread (along with special treats for these solitary days, such as a hoarded terrine of pâté de foie

gras and a jar of preserved kumquats). In the icebox a reserve
of two or three varieties of cheese is always on hand throughout the winter. In the cellar wait preserves, wine, chili sauces,
a bag of potatoes, another of onions. And I feel it unwise ever
to be without a cabbage and a rutabaga around the house during these winter months of possible cataclysm.

The Blizzard Cupboard is a custom since adopted by many
of my city friends who live in small apartments without a deep
freeze. A blizzard may not be so confining in town as in the
country; yet there are days when one suddenly decides one
simply does not want to go shopping, when even a light winter
drizzle can seem forbidding. Or raging hunger might grip you
at three in the morning. A date unexpectedly be canceled. A
cold keep the solitary dweller confined. Or, could be, you just
feel plain lazy.

But the purpose of the Blizzard Cupboard is not merely to
have a store of food on hand nor must the variety be great;
its purpose is also to have an imaginative *combination* of
canned goods so that life, at least at the dinner table, need not
be dull though the roads are blocked and shops seem a hun-
dred miles away. Canned goods need not be altogether scorned
by good cooks if they are used with taste and reason. Heated
as they come from the can, commercial foods are too often
dreary. But pea soup, tomato soup, some bouillon made from
cubes, and a can of crab meat or lobster and a jigger of sherry
will blend to a delicious bisque. A can of chili, spaghetti and
button mushrooms (these browned first in butter along with
onions), mixed in a casserole with a dash of this or that sauce,
topped with Parmesan cheese and bacon strips and baked for
half an hour, makes a dinner not to be served without honor.

The dishes described below, all excellent, can be called

forth from a square foot of hoarded supplies on anyone's kitchen shelf. It's using the head that counts.

❧ PORK-FRIED RICE

For this, a can of any of the good pork luncheon meats is always kept on hand. Chop 2 medium onions very fine and fry them gently in 3 T butter about 5 minutes, not letting them brown. If you have a little green pepper, chop this and fry along with the onions, plus a handful of fresh celery leaves, or some dried celery flakes or a piece of chopped celery root. Then add 1 cup of water, bring to a boil and dissolve in it 2 chicken bouillon cubes. Now add 3 cups of cooked, drained rice, 1 cup luncheon meat cut into narrow inch-long sticks, a dash of Worcestershire, salt to taste and a generous amount of freshly ground pepper. Heat through, not letting it burn. The mixture should be moist but have no liquid remaining in the pan, and don't let the rice become mushy. If possible, add at the last moment a cup of finely shredded lettuce and cook only long enough to wilt the lettuce. Remove from the fire, and stir in a whole raw egg—don't shun this, for the heat of the mixture will solidify the egg sufficiently as it coats all the rice kernels. Top with a sprinkling of burned slivered almonds or raisins before serving; for an accompaniment, try a salad of fresh or canned tart fruits.

❧ LENTILS AND LUNCHEON MEAT

Chop a medium onion and 1 clove garlic and fry lightly in 3 T butter. Add 2 cups quick-cooking lentils, 1 bayleaf and 6 peppercorns, cover with water and simmer only until just tender. Add a small can of drained boiled onions, 1 t wet mustard, ¼ t dried thyme or orégano, salt and pepper to taste. Line a baking dish with slices of luncheon meat or a small canned ham. Pour the lentils and their liquor over the meat; then pour over this ¾ cup either of canned consommé, red wine or beer. Top with bacon slices and bake half an hour in a moderate oven until the bacon is crisp. Serve with a bowl of onion rings marinated in, French dressing.

৪৯ CORN AND RICE AU GRATIN

Combine a can of creamed corn with a cup of cooked rice, 3 beaten egg yolks, 2 chopped canned pimentos, a small chopped onion, 1 t salt, 1 T melted butter and ½ t paprika. Turn half into a buttered casserole, cover with a layer of mild grated cheese such as Swiss or Provelone, pour in remaining half of corn mixture and cover with another layer of grated cheese. Dot with butter or small squares of bacon; bake in a very hot oven for 15 or 20 minutes. This is a good luncheon dish. With it, serve roasted canned Vienna (or other) sausages; we roast them before the open fire and let the blizzard entomb the house.

৪৯ CANNED CORNED BEEF WITH CABBAGE

Cabbages, of course, will keep well in a cool place during the winter and supply a taste of freshness when other green vegetables are lacking. Prepare fried green cabbage (see page 97) being careful not to allow it to overcook. Have a can of corned beef chilled so that it will slice without crumbling (the Argentina tinned corned beef has an excellent flavor). Cut into ¼" slices, place on top of the cooked cabbage, cover, and steam over low heat just long enough to heat the meat through. Dish onto a warm platter, surround with boiled, buttered potatoes, and you'll think summer has returned. A wine and mustard sauce will add zest to the meat.

ᙇ WINE AND MUSTARD SAUCE
Combine a jar of wet mustard with a jar of currant jelly in equal parts and lace with either port or claret wine to taste. This will keep a long while if kept chilled.

During the long winter months here in the country, I never cook a company roast or stew in fair weather without making sure that enough will be left over to supply at least one emergency meal should storms blow up during the night (since home-cooked meats are, after all, more inviting than canned). From these leftovers, savory dishes have evolved, augmented by the treasures of the Blizzard Cupboard, to be enjoyed in contentment while outside new snow fell. . . .

ᙇ SPAGHETTI FROM LEFTOVER BEEF
Put the leftover pieces of beef roast or stew through a meat grinder. For a heaping cupful or so of ground meat, also grind a large onion, 1 or 2 cloves of garlic to taste and, should you have any, a stick of celery, some green pepper and parsley. Fry this mixture until golden brown in 4 T butter or olive oil. Add the juice of half a lemon, a can of mushrooms with their liquor, a can of tomato purée or sauce, ½ t dried sweet basil, a bay leaf, 1 t Worcestershire, a pinch of ground allspice, salt and pepper to taste. Now add any leftover gravy there may be, strained, plus canned consommé or beef bouillon cubes dissolved in water to make 2 cups of liquid in all. A few pulverized anchovies are a good addition as well as ½ cup red wine. Simmer for at least an hour and taste; if necessary, add more consommé or bouillon, for the flavor should

be more that of a meat sauce than of the usual tomato sauce. Cook longer if need be; during the last 10 minutes add 1 t Kitchen Bouquet and when the sauce is rich and thick serve over spaghetti with Parmesan cheese.

ࣆ CHOP SUEY FROM LEFTOVER ROAST

You'll find this an agreeable way to use any leftover roast—beef, pork or veal—or leftover steak or fowl. Cut the meat into thin, narrow strips. For each generous cupful of the meat, cook a large chopped onion in 3 T butter for 5 minutes without letting it brown. Add dried celery flakes, if you have no fresh. (Celery, however, if well sealed in wax paper, will keep well over several weeks in the refrigrator; therefore, I always have it on hand for salads, stews, appetizers or to use the leaves and roots as necessary flavoring in soups.) If you have the fresh celery, cut several stalks diagonally into narrow, inch-and-a-half spears. Add to the onion, along with a cup of water and 2 chicken bouillon cubes, fresh pepper, 1 t Kitchen Bouquet and 1 T soy sauce; simmer covered only until the celery can be pierced with a fork—it should remain quite crisp. Add the meat and a can of drained mixed Chinese vegetables, salt and additional soy sauce to taste, as well as more water or bouillon if needed; heat through only. Thicken the liquid with cornstarch. Serve on a bed of chow mein noodles, heated in the oven until crisp, and with steamed rice.

ࣆ POOR MAN'S STROGANOFF

Though leftover rib roast, rump or steak are excellent for this, I particularly enjoy using leftover pot roast, creating such elegant fare from such a humble cut. Trim all the fat from the meat and slice it very thin—across the grain, if pot roast is used. For 1 lb. of sliced meat, fry a small diced onion in butter or fresh bacon fat until light gold. Add a medium can of drained button mushrooms if your larder provides no fresh; if it does, use ¼ lb. of them, previously browned in butter. Next add ½ cup leftover gravy, ½ cup water, ½ cup red wine and a bouillon cube. If there is no leftover gravy, substitute an additional ½ cup wine and 1 t Kitchen Bouquet. Then comes 4 T tomato sauce or 2 T tomato paste, ½ t dry mustard, ½ t Worcestershire, and 1 minced clove of garlic. Simmer the sauce for 10 or 15 minutes until it is reduced and slightly thickened. Add the meat, heat through only, and stir in half a cup of sour cream, which is another of those valued aids that will survive a week or more in the icebox. Heap this delicious Stroganoff around a mound of wild rice and garnish with dill pickles or unpeeled cucumber sticks.

With such dinners awaiting me, all through the planned prodigality of the Blizzard Cupboard, I no longer fear the sudden, devilish dumping of snow from the sky. It is fun to outwit nature; instead of apprehension, I know now that the howling sheet of white outside will only increase the delights I have learned to find in a country kitchen.

❀

CHAPTER FOUR
_____

A COUNTRY KITCHEN

_____

WHAT SHOULD A country kitchen be?

I can speak only of my own and my own wants. It must be big, at least reasonably so, to attain again its rightful place as core of the home, accommodating life like an overflowing basket. Here a long sweep of windows looks over the sink past a dooryard garden down the hill to a stand of junipers and yellow maples. From another wall, windows look out to an arbored terrace and grapevines and a single pear tree.

There is a fireplace in the kitchen and a mission oak table, refinished and bleached, capable of stretching out to seat sixteen; but more than dining is done here. It is a table for playing cards, or to sprawl over while reading a dozen new seed catalogues, or to sit around with neighbors drinking beer or coffee. Parties always end up around it. It is also there to hold several dozen quart-jars and a few laden bushel baskets and dripping ladles during pickling time. It won't stain, either.

I like to remember my mother's respect for her kitchen: it was a kind of holy place from which she ministered lavishly to her family via stove and sink and cupboards and flour bin. There were rag rugs on the floor; usually wild white daisies or goldenrod stuck in a milk bottle, or garden flowers (her favorite bunch was of snow-on-the-mountain and small deep red dahlias); and almost always a rolling pin or flour sifter or earthenware mixing bowl was in sight. Here also she made root beer each year, which never failed to explode a month later, rocking the walls of the fruit cellar and shattering nearby jars of jams and Slippery Slims.

She would have looked with smiling placidity, but inward scorn and despair for her sex, at today's houswives, who are helpless without packaged pie crust and canned potato salad and precooked rice and who deem it a chore to simmer day-long an honest soup, depriving themselves of its aromatic pleasure. Good cooking was a way of life and enjoyment. You did not save time but spent it recklessly, proudly, and with full reward inside these four spotless walls.

It is a good way to feel toward one's kitchen. In ours, the love of eating does not abate before the dinner dishes are washed; we sit there afterward with friends reading old cookbooks, enjoying the offhand splendor of an old German book, *Wir nimmen zwoelf Eier* . . . we take twelve eggs, indeed! Or the steely imagination of Isabella Beeton, who was to Victorian England what Fanny Farmer was to America, and who makes no bones about "Toast Sandwich, How to Make"—butter two pieces of bread and place a neatly trimmed slice of toast between them! No shilly-shallying for Isabella. Though for variety, she adds, a piece of pulled meat may be added. Whichever, she orders it to be placed on a "d'oyley" and sent to table at once.

Or my neighbor Connie Smith drops in with a frayed, handwritten recipe book revealing directions for brewing a concoction of hops, malt and yeast; this elixir bears the title of "Beverage," penciled there by her paternal grandmother who apparently did not intend to let her right hand know what her spirit was enjoying. My maternal grandmother was more forthright. In *her* recipe book there is a cure for diarrhea which begins, "Take one gallon best brandy. . . ."

And in our kitchen the seasons are always present: in a basket of freshly gathered wild asparagus or dandelions or in the year's first peas; then in the glory of dill and later in the comfort of squashes; then in the butternuts and black walnuts and a partridge and winter soups and at last the pickled herring salad for New Year's Eve. You notice one evening that the days have grown longer, a new light hangs in the sky, the wiry willows have brightened their yellows. It is spring again.

Here in this kitchen you also sit around dreaming up perfect combinations of herb and vegetable and fowl and beast to make perfect food, as I have tried to do in this book.

INDEX